OUR
CANADA

CLB 845
Copyright ©1987 Colour Library Books Ltd., Guildford, Surrey, England.
Illustrations pages 40, 41, 239 bottom, 240 top, 243,
    273, 362 top: copyright © 1987 Parks Canada.
Text filmsetting by Acesetters Ltd., Richmond, Surrey, England.
Printed and bound in Barcelona, Spain by Cronion, S.A.
All rights reserved.
ISBN 0 86283 391 4
Dep. Leg. B-12.683-87

OUR
CANADA

Text by
Peter N. Casey

COOMBE BOOKS

CONTENTS

Horse-powered log cutting at the Kings Landing Historical Settlement, New Brunswick.

Previous pages: glacier-fed Peyto Lake (left), in Alberta, and the ice canoe race across the St. Lawrence during Quebec's "Carnaval" winter festival (right).

Introduction

For Canadians, as well as for visitors from other lands, it is the eye, like a camera, and the memory, like an album of favourite photographs, that best describe this giant country we call Canada, that finally create a perfect picture of the whole.

For some, Canada is sunrise breaking through the fog in a small Newfoundland harbour, an iceberg floating off the coast in the middle of June. Others tell us that you can never truly know what Canada is until you have felt the tug of an Atlantic salmon on your line while standing waist deep in the cold spring waters of the St. Mary's River in Nova Scotia. There are people from outside the country who remember Canada as a winding, leisurely motor trip through the pastoral landscape along the St. John River in New Brunswick, or an outing at a church supper on Prince Edward Island where every guest was served a two-pound lobster. Some say Canada is the magnificent scenery of Quebec's Gaspé coast, the quaintness of Quebec City, or the bustling activity in the streets of Montreal. Canada is all of this, and more.

For some, Canada is day-to-day life in a small rural town in Ontario, a visit to the nation's capital city of Ottawa during the annual tulip festival, or taking in the sights and sounds of the country's largest metropolis, Toronto, where two-and-a-half-million Canadians make their homes.

Canada is a drive across the ocean of wheat fields that are the Canadian prairies, a train ride through the unbelievably magnificent Rocky Mountains, or sunset on Long Beach on the west coast of Vancouver Island.

To describe a country that stretches across six time zones, from the Atlantic to the Pacific Ocean, and then again from the North Pole halfway to the Equator, where the land ranges from fertile, grassy farmlands or frozen tundra to the tops of some of the tallest mountains on the continent, and where summertime temperatures can be as hot as the tropics or as cold as 50° below zero, is no small challenge. It is no wonder, then, that the 25 million people who inhabit the almost 4 million square miles of Canada, prefer instead to describe the country in terms of their favourite places and favourite things to do.

As could be expected in the second-largest nation in the world, those lists are long.

If a picture, indeed, is worth a thousand words, then the many brilliantly produced colour plates within the pages of this book will tell you the story of Canada as it has seldom, if ever, been told before.

From east to west, from north to south, they tell the vivid story of contrasts that dazzle the eye, that – once you have seen them – remain in the memory forever. Here are the broad, bold strokes of the canvas of the Canadian landscapes – the frantic cities, the lonely, tranquil country roads, the ever-mysterious forests, and the carefully sculpted gardens of city parks.

From the harbours of British Columbia to the island fortress of Newfoundland, from the Point Pelee marshlands in Ontario, the most southerly spot in Canada, to the Canadian arctic islands surrounding the North Pole, barely a mile of Canada is quite the same as the one before. It is this ever-challenging, ever-changing panorama, perhaps, that best defines the country as a whole.

As our American neighbours to the south are apt to report, and as the seasons of the Canadian year seem intent on proving, Canada is where the weather is made. Canadians, who are said to talk about the weather more than any other people in the world, would hasten to add that it is seldom made to order.

The seasons come and go in Canada in splendid style. In this country, in fact, it is sometimes possible to find at least three out of the four coming or going at the same time.

In March, for instance, when the arctic tundra plains lie frozen under the 24-hour darkness of the northern sky, and grumbling Torontonians begin to count the days to spring, that mysterious wind Canadians call the Chinook races out of the Rocky Mountains, raises the temperature by as much as 60 degrees Fahrenheit, and blesses the city of Calgary with spring in three hours flat. But wait, there's more!

In March, in Vancouver, flower gardens are in full bloom, and office workers spend their lunch hours tanning in the parks. In March, in a good year, this city has been practising *summer* for almost a month, and businessmen just arrived from the east try vainly to pretend that the winter coats over their arms are on their way to the dry cleaners.

The colour of Canada in autumn is more than a memory. It is nature's annual sound and light show with the sound turned down, a happy fireworks of scarlet reds, yellows, oranges, and even browns that decorate mountain ranges, rolling hills, wilderness forests and city parks, backyards and neighbourhoods from one side of the country to the other. Once you have seen it, it becomes a part of you.

With so much weather, and faced with the fact that grinning and bearing it – or enjoying it – are the only choices, it is not surprising that Canadians work hard at the business of putting it to perfect use, and that in every season people from other countries visit to join in the fun.

Here is skiing in the Quebec Laurentians, in the Gatineaus to the north of Ottawa, or on the incredible downhill Rocky Mountain slopes of Alberta and British Columbia.

Here is yachting on both coasts, and boating on those inland seas we call the Great Lakes.

Here too are the lakes, rivers, and streams that attract sportsfishermen from around the world.

Canada is all of this, and more.

For Canadians then, and for visitors from other lands, *Our Canada* is the story of people – at home, at work, at play – in every province, and at every time of the year.

Canada... a place to live, a place to visit, a place to dream about.

Lobster traps on the shores of the Gaspé Peninsula, Quebec.

BRITISH COLUMBIA, YUKON AND NORTHWEST TERRITORIES

If the original visitors to Canada had waited for Captain James Cook to lead the way, or for Captain George Vancouver, and settlement had happened west-to-east instead of the other way around, the country would bear little resemblance to the one we know today. For having reached British Columbia, say the people who live there now, our forebears would have had precious little reason to *eastward ho!*, and Canada, beyond its Rocky Mountain backdrop, would have remained largely uninhabited.

But this, of course, was not to be. For in 1792, when Captain Vancouver was sent by the King of England to survey and claim this great western territory – a mere 14 years after Cook had first dropped anchor – settlement was already burgeoning in the east, and a westward march of adventurers was on its way to meet him.

Today they continue to come, from across Canada and from around the world; adventurers of a new age, a new kind, not seeking the fortunes of the fur trade, nor those of gold and silver, but for a wealth of other reasons which, even the people who live here year-round will tell you, can never be taken for granted.

To the visitor approaching British Columbia from the east, west, north, or south, the Canadian Rockies loom a welcome unmatched by any other mark on the Canadian landscape. Hugging the coastline from the Yukon and Alaska in the north, southward to the Canada-U.S. border, protecting the inhabitants of this Pacific province from even the seasons as we know them in the rest of Canada, they challenge the imagination of the first-time visitor. Seen from the prairie flatness, for a time at least, they are the grandest of illusions, rising suddenly from the rolling Alberta foothills – breathtaking, massive, postcard-perfect. "Look!" shouts the traveller, "the Rockies! Just up ahead!" later to discover, as they grow larger and larger on the horizon, that they are still many hours and many miles away.

From the air, there is no illusion. Wave after wave, range after range of snow-capped, granite peaks hide between them lush and forested valleys as incredibly deep as these mountains are high. Within this range lie the headwaters of the legendary Fraser, Thompson, Peace, Athabaska, Mackenzie, Kamloops, and Columbia Rivers. Here, in this *Great Divide*, and from the Columbia Icefield, rivers more robust and spectacular than any in North America begin to carve the routes that will take them eventually to the Pacific, the Arctic and even, through Hudson Bay, to the Atlantic Ocean.

Here, in comfort, the modern-day air traveller marvels at the rise and fall of a forested, primeval landscape stretching in all directions as far as the eye can see; or – at unbelievable altitudes – is startled by the sudden appearance of monstrous, island-like peaks jutting above the cloud cover and into the sky.

It is through these mountains, in the wake of Alexander Mackenzie, that subsequent waves of explorers, adventurers, fur traders and, later, teams of surveyors and engineers, charted routes of their own; routes travelled today by many hundreds of thousands of travellers along the highways and railways that link British Columbia with the rest of Canada.

As with all things western, the Canadian Rockies are arguably at their most splendid when viewed from the west. It is here, from the Pacific, that they rise more sharply, more dramatically, than from any other point of view. As if built where they are solely for the wonderment and visual delight of the people along this coast, they stand in stark and monumental contrast to the everyday, sea-level life below. Seen from the eastern shores of Vancouver Island, from the pre-occupied bustle of busy Vancouver streetcorners, or from cocktail and dining lounges atop the city's downtown, highrise hotels, the mountains seem to shout their climb into the western skies: snow-capped, whiter-than-white, dazzling in the afternoon sun. Still other times, as if to prove their role in at least the coastal nature of things, they match their sweep and height against the elements themselves, shielding this city of bays and beaches from arctic air, or blocking the eastward passage of wind and rain-filled clouds for days on end.

The third-largest city in Canada, Vancouver, like the province of British Columbia itself, is a mini-world of striking contrasts. Here, sheltered from the unpredictable Pacific by Vancouver Island, private and public gardens bloom while much of the rest of the country bundles itself against the bitter chills of February and March and counts the seemingly endless days to spring. Here, throughout most of the winter and spring, the golf courses, public beaches, tennis courts, and yachting and sailing clubs are as busy as the snow-covered ski trails on nearby mountain slopes.

Here, annually, some 16,000 coastal and ocean-going vessels visit the more than 100 miles of shoreline in the harbours and inlets of Georgia Strait, making Vancouver the largest and busiest seaport on the Pacific coast of North America. With the mountains and the rest of Canada at its back, Vancouver looks north, south, and east at the world around it. For the almost one-and-a-quarter million people who live in Canada's "Gateway to the Orient," Tokyo is closer, by more than 300 miles, than is Halifax on Canada's other coast. And despite the railway links that eventually welded this province to Confederation in 1885, discussion of business interests in "the East" – more often than not – refers to the Far East here.

More than one million people visit this most beautiful of Canadian cities every year. And while many come to cluster in boardrooms on matters of national and international importance, many more come to vacation, stopping off for several days during larger explorations of the natural wonders of the province, or holidaying in the city itself.

Called "the city of bays and bridges" or, alternatively, "the city of neighbourhoods," Vancouver is unmistakably and indisputably both: its geography – those very "neighbourhoods" – surrounded, interrupted, and enhanced by water at every turn. To the north, North and West Vancouver are linked across Burrard Inlet with Burnaby and downtown Vancouver by

Husky dog team and musher on Baffin Island, Northwest Territories.

the Second Narrows, and the Lion's Gate Bridge. On the northeast, visitors to Vancouver's 1,000-acre Stanley Park can watch the comings and goings of ships in Georgia Strait, or gaze across English Bay toward the magnificently landscaped grounds of the University of British Columbia. At the head of English Bay, False Creek wanders into the city, where tiny harbour tugs and pleasure craft chug back and forth, and seagulls squawk for handouts under the spans of the Granville Island Bridge. Still further south, the Fraser River cuts its final, lazy swath toward the sea, close by the satellite communities of New Westminister and Sea Island (where Vancouver's airport is located).

As the province of British Columbia is to backpackers and hikers, the city of Vancouver, for people who enjoy such things, is a walker's paradise. Here, within easy reach of the downtown core, are miles of waterfront, unbelievably deserted stretches of sandy beach, and more than 150 public parks. Vancouver, too, boasts the second largest Chinatown in North America (next to San Francisco's), its streets a busy maze of shops, shoppers, and restaurants. The Nitobe Memorial Gardens, overlooking English Bay near the University of British Columbia's sprawling campus, is the finest display of Japanese gardening techniques in all of Canada.

For an evening stroll, the lively streets of Gastown are a must. This is where the city began. In the 1860s its nighttime streets were a-howl with the yells and shouts of lumberjacks from the nearby mills. Today they are alive with the laughter and conversation of the young, chic men-and-women-about-town who come here to shop, drink, dine, dance, and listen to music in the boutiques, antique shops, restaurants, and nightclubs.

For most holidaying families, no visit to this seaport city is complete without a day spent exploring the many wonders of Stanley Park, where giant stands of hemlock, cedar, and Douglas fir offer a dramatic glimpse of how this forested shoreline must have looked more than a century ago. Here the young and young-at-heart can wander miles of woodland trails amid the sights and sounds of the natural world. The park – the largest natural preserve in any city on the continent – also contains a zoo of more than 500 species of animals from this country and from around the globe. Here too, the Vancouver Public Aquarium is home to more than 8000 marine animals, including killer whales. And, certainly worthy of mention in the same breath with natural phenomena, the visitor will also find giant totem poles carved by coastal Indians in another time.

In Stanley Park it is possible to forget that the city exists, and visitors can be forgiven for occasionally having to remind themselves that its busy streets and sidewalks are but minutes away.

As the Canadian Rockies are best viewed from this coast and from this city, it is entirely appropriate that the grandest overall view of this sprawling metropolis, in turn, is from the mountains. And, as is the case with Stanley Park, very few people who visit this city leave without at least one trip to nearby Grouse Mountain. Here, Canada's largest aerial tramway travels skyward 3700 feet up the mountainside to the top for a panoramic

view in all directions of the city, the harbor, the neighbouring mountains, and the eastern shore of Vancouver Island across the Georgia Strait.

It has often been said that to see the *British* in British Columbia, one need only pay a visit to Vancouver Island and the city of Victoria at its southern tip. If indeed there is a time and a place for everything here, we may be assured, the time is Victorian, and the place is Victoria, where nostalgia is a way of life. Here in the capital of British Columbia, oddly and quite properly aloof from the banter and bickering of parliamentary debate, tradition lives; and on a single day's outing the visitor is greeted by myriad images that speak of things the way they *ought to be*. Victoria's tourists can catch double-decker buses or horse-drawn *tallyho* carriages along civilized, unhurried streets. They can browse the tidy shops for English tweeds and fine bone china. Rose gardens and holly hedges surround the grounds of stately mansions, and flowers bloom throughout the year. The bemused visitor can pause to watch lawn bowlers, or take in a cricket match, or stop for high tea at the ivy-covered Empress Hotel. For bird watchers, there is the thrill of spotting a meadowlark in a downtown park; the birds were introduced to the Island from England in 1903.

Beyond the quaintness and civility of Victoria, the breathtaking natural beauty of Vancouver Island lies in all directions. To the west, overlooking Juan de Fuca Strait and the Pacific, is Pacific Rim National Park, one of five national parks in the province.

Here visitors can dig for clams, marvel at the variety and abundance of migrating wildfowl attracted by the tidal pools and mudflats, explore sea caves, and comb miles of surf-battered shoreline for the flotsam and jetsam of the Pacific. Here, from Long Beach, boat tours are available to Sea Lion Rocks where Steller's sea lions bask in the sun. And here too, visitors can probe the shadowy wonders of the rain forest where grow the largest trees in the world.

From the villages of Bamfield and Tofino, on Vancouver Island's west coast, tour boats take visitors off shore to watch schools of gray whales making their way up the coast to their summer feeding grounds in the Bering Sea. On the east coast, at Telegraph Cove, you can sail amidst the antics of killer whales.

In the mountains and along the Island's coastline, giant bald eagles and osprey soar in their daily hunt for food, as indeed they do throughout British Columbia.

From Victoria to its northern tip, almost 300 miles away, Vancouver Island boasts such a variety of scenery and lifestyle that, in fact, many have come to regard it as Canada's Pacific paradise. Visitors from all across the country and from foreign lands as well make plans to retire here, and many do. Still others, apparently, come for a visit and simply stay on. High tea at the Empress and year-round Pacific temperatures aside, the Island, as it is commonly called, has much to offer.

In the rugged interior, deer and wild elk graze, indifferent to the camera-toting tourists in Strathcona Provincial Park. Wolves, wolverine and cougar live here too. At

Campbell River, on the northeast coast, sportsfishermen will tell you that too few places in the world provide salmon of such fight and quality.

Everywhere, the Island is marked by trout-filled lakes and streams, and blessed with rich farmland and Eden-like forests where 600-year-old Douglas firs climb more than 200 feet toward the sun and sky. At Strathcona, you can see in the distance the peak of Mount Golden Hind rising more that 7200 feet above sea level. Everywhere, the land is near the sea.

From Beacon Hill Park in downtown Victoria, the view is of Juan de Fuca Strait, and, on a clear day, the Olympic Mountains of Washington State. On the west coast, the ever-moody, ever-changing Pacific throws gentle waves, booming surf, or violent, storm-tossed breakers against the land. To the north looking toward the sombre beauty of the Queen Charlotte Islands, celebrated in the timeless painting of Emily Carr, one sees the Pacific again.

From Victoria, in season, you can ferry to Seattle, Washington. From Commox, on the Island's eastern shore, a ferry service runs to Powell River on the British Columbia mainland. From Port Hardy in the north, ferries make the long and scenic trip through Georgia Strait, then up the rugged mainland coast to Prince Rupert, from where further boat service provides access to the Queen Charlotte Islands, or further north to Alaska. Vancouver and Victoria are linked by ferry service twelve months of the year.

At Nanaimo, the second largest community on Vancouver Island, and once a prominent trading post for the Hudson's Bay Company, thousands of tourists, locals, and daredevils gather every July for mayhem and boating of a uniquely special kind – the annual *Nanaimo-to-Vancouver Bathtub Race*!

British Columbia, it would seem, is in fact a uniquely special kind of province at every turn.

For sailors and power boat enthusiasts, the very coastline demands exploration, be it afternoon or weeks-long trips. For skiers, Grouse Mountain and the magnificent slopes of Whistler, both within easy driving distance of the city of Vancouver, offer every degree of thrill, difficulty, and pleasure imaginable, while Glacier National Park and myriad other mountains and slopes reachable only by helicopter are covered with the virgin snows that only the maddest hotdoggers and dreamers dare to imagine.

For whitewater rafters, British Columbia rivers are legendary... the Fraser, Columbia, Lillooet... the Kamloops, Kootenay, and Thompson. Fishing and hunting areas of the province are among the most famous on the continent, and British Columbia game fish and big game trophies are the prized possessions of fishermen and hunters around the world. For hikers and backpackers, this larger-than-Texas province of mountains, valleys, shoreline, and unspoiled wilderness, contains five of Canada's most magnificent national parks.

∗ Pacific Rim National Park, on the western shore of Vancouver Island, has a rain forest at its back, and the Pacific Ocean sweeping its miles of tidal beaches and driftwood-strewn coves.

∗ Mount Revelstoke National Park, close by the town of the same name (which serves as the jumping-off point for all of the national parks on the mainland) is 100 square miles of mountain peaks, glaciers, streams and forest. Situated some 8000 feet above sea level, the park is world-renowned for its championship ski runs.

∗ In Glacier National Park, between Revelstoke and Rogers Pass – frequently called the most beautiful mountain highway in the world – mountain peaks soar beyond 11,000 feet and glaciers and icefields tempt the truly professional skiers with breathtaking downhill runs up to four miles long.

∗ At Yoho National Park you'll have little trouble accepting the English translation of the park's Indian name. Yoho literally means "wow!" or "spectacular" and all who visit here agree. In this park, just to the west of the great Continental Divide, close to 300 miles of hiking and horseback trails traverse the more than 500 square miles of unbelievable scenery. At Yoho, visitors marvel at the mysteriously shaped stone pillars in Hoodoo Valley, the majesty of Yoho Glacier, and the 1200-foot plunge of Takakkaw Falls.

∗ At Kootenay National Park visitors can visit Marble Canyon or treat themselves to a therapeutic dip in the hot mineral pools at Radium Springs.

For campers and the holidayers with mobile homes, miles of excellent highway lead into the magnificent ranching country, farmland, and orchards of the Okanagan Valley, into the Kootenay region, and further north into Cariboo country.

Prince Rupert, after Vancouver, is the province's largest, busiest, and most important port. Its year-round facilities are home-base to a large and prosperous fishing fleet; its harbour, as the western terminus of the Canadian National Railway, is bustling with the traffic of grain carriers come to carry Canadian prairie wheat to the four corners of the world. With an annual catch of more than 18 million pounds, Prince Rupert has deservedly earned its name as the Halibut Capital of the World. From here, the northern reaches, the interior farmlands, and the vast lumbering areas of the province can be reached by boat, rail, automobile, and, of course, by plane.

From here you can take the coastal ferry ride to the southern tip of the Alaska Panhandle, or turn into the interior to Prince George and onto Dawson Creek on the Alberta border. At Dawson Creek, the famed Alaska Highway begins its 1,523-mile northern route through British Columbia's Peace River country, into the Yukon, and onto Fairbanks, Alaska.

At Prince Rupert, it is said, the visitor breaks his bonds with Vancouver, Victoria, and the densely populated areas of the southern part of the province, and turns his back on the pastoral landscapes of the south. At Prince Rupert, if the visitor is going to feel or hear it anywhere, the mysterious lure of the north is strongly evident.

For those seeking a truly wilderness experience, northern British Columbia, and the Yukon beyond, offer the stuff of which dreams are made. A rugged, mountainous land criss-crossed by spectacular rivers and streams – for those who love the untamed out-of-doors, it is an unspoiled paradise. Deer, moose, elk, caribou, and mountain sheep roam the land. Arctic char, salmon, steelhead trout, grayling, and northern pike are the bountiful harvest of its many waterways and lakes. For many people who have never visited Canada, in fact, the Yukon and the Northwest Territories stretching eastward across the top of Canada are the legend and image that southern Canadians have long sought to dispel.

This is the landscape that foreign film makers and photographers cannot resist, and which residents of this "Land of the Midnight Sun" do much to promote. From the border of Alaska in the west to the stormy Atlantic Ocean, from the 60th parallel of latitude to the North Pole, this is "The Top of the World".

In the Yukon, the mecca for more than 80,000 adventurers following the gold rush of 1896, roughly 25,000 people remain, surrounded by the ghosts and legends celebrated in the stories of Jack London, and the poetry of Robert Service.

One of the coldest areas in Canada, if not in the world, the Yukon, like the Northwest Territories, enjoys the extremes of 24-hour darkness and sunlight. In summer, it is possible under such extremes and in backyard gardens to grow cabbage, squash, or pumpkins of impossible size; in winter, if it should be desirable, one can sleep for 24-hours at a time beneath the blackness and the dancing shards of the northern lights.

In Dawson City, the centre of the gold rush and pandemonium that opened this inhospitable land, fewer than 400 hearty souls remain among the memories and relics of those boom years. And here, in what was once heralded as the "Paris of the North," visitors, with the help of spirited, local entrepreneurs, can sample the lifestyle that bloomed when this town was home-base to more than 40,000 prospectors, miners and the gaggle of adventurers who followed them here. Today's tourists can buy sourdough bread, sup and dine in the clapboard taverns, wander the decks of restored riverboats, play roulette and toast the can-can dancers in local saloons, and visit the cabin where Robert Service penned the ballads that continue to celebrate the memory of days long gone. Here too, where vast fortunes were hauled from single claims, visitors can still arrange to pan for gold along Bonanza and Eldorado creeks.

Gold is still important to the Yukon – close to $20 million dollars worth of ore is mined annually – but the concept of the lonely, hermit-like prospectors has all but disappeared, replaced today by the huge mining conglomerates that harvest the land of its riches of gold, silver, copper, lead, and zinc.

South of Dawson City, on the banks of the Yukon River, is Whitehorse, the capital of this sprawling northern territory. Readily accessible by road, and by air from Vancouver and Edmonton, it is a bustling metropolis of some 15,000 inhabitants. In addition to being the centre of government, Whitehorse is also the historical headquarters of the legendary North West Mounted Police.

One hundred miles east of Whitehorse is Kluane National Park, an 850-square-mile preserve of forest, lakes, streams, and alpine meadows dominated by Mount Logan – Canada's highest mountain, at 19,850 feet (6055 metres).

For the visitor, everything seems a bit larger than life in the Yukon – the mountains, the stories, and even the climate. In summer, the days grow as hot as in Hawaii; in winter, local wags will tell you, conversations have been known to freeze in the air, the words and stories unspoken, unthawed, until spring.

Fewer than 70,000 people inhabit the almost two-million square miles that make up the Yukon and the Northwest Territories. This population includes the original inhabitants – the Inuit and peoples of the great Dene nation – as well as the travellers and adventurers of this and other lands, people possessed of the peculiar pioneer spirit with which wildernesses and frontiers are broken. In Dawson City, Whitehorse, Yellowknife, Inuvik, Tuktoyaktuk, or Frobisher Bay, it is often said that it is impossible to gather a crowd that cannot trace its roots to the four corners of the globe.

For the most part, the Northwest Territories is a barren, rocky plateau, left scarred and treeless by retreating glaciers of the Ice Age. Where vegetation exists, it does so in the form of stunted, stubborn greenery. The Yukon, on the other hand, its southwestern corner warmed by the Pacific, its Rocky Mountain valleys sheltered from the arctic winds, is lush and green throughout much of the year. But barren or treed, populated or echo-empty, one visit to either of these great northern territories will soon convince the outsider of the reasons why the people who live here would not consider trading their lifestyle for any other in the world.

In the Northwest Territories herds of up to 100,000 caribou move with the seasons in search of grazing grounds. Polar bears roam the arctic ice in search of prey; occasionally, lured by the waste and smells of civilization, they wander into populated towns. High in the Arctic, herds of musk oxen feed on the grasses and lichen that arctic islands afford, and band into protective circles when approached by predator or man. For the adventurous photographer, the entire northland is a wildlife dream come true. Moose graze at every bend along the Mackenzie River valley. Grizzlies and black bears roam the mountains to the west. Arctic wolves, hare, fox, and wolverines all make their homes here, and throughout the brief arctic summer the skies are alive with flocks of migrating ducks, geese, and other birds.

With its miles of accessible highways, the romantic history of the gold rush, and the marvels of Kluane National Park, the Yukon has long been a favourite destination of holidayers bent on "getting away from it all." For the Northwest Territories, however, tourism is a relatively new industry, but one that continues to grow each year as intrepid, modern day explorers return home to boast of the wonders of this vast and magnificent frontier. Kluane National Park, for instance, provides an astonishing view of Mount Robson – at 12,972 feet (3954 metres), the highest peak in the Canadian Rockies.

At Fort Smith, summer visitors can enjoy white water rafting on the Slave River, or join excursions into Wood Buffalo National Park, the second largest park in the world. Wood Buffalo is the only known nesting ground of the whooping crane, and it is also home to 2000 buffalo – the largest free ranging herd in the world.

From Fort Simpson you can, with guides, explore the mystical canyons of the legendary Nahanni River, or travel the historic Mackenzie River all the way to the Arctic Ocean.

Yellowknife, the capital of the Northwest Territories, is a take-off point for arctic adventure of every kind. Great Slave Lake and Great Bear Lake are reachable by float plane, and teeming with trophy-sized lake trout and great northern pike. Streams and rivers in all directions are rich with grayling. From Yellowknife, in the spring and fall, a one-hour flight will take you over a sea of migrating caribou.

Further north, at the mouth of the Mackenzie River, and within 80 miles of the Arctic Ocean, are the communities of Tuktoyaktuk, Inuvik and Aklavik where the southern visitor can shop for Inuit art and handicraft or, in the company of native guides, visit the edge of the Arctic Ocean to view whales and seals at "The Top Of The World."

"Inuvik," say the people who live here, "is not the end of the world, but you can see it from here!"

The Canadian Arctic, the Yukon, and the Northwest Territories combined stretch across the tops of all but the Atlantic Provinces, and make up close to one-half of the country's land mass. Here, more than a million lakes, rivers, and streams contain more than one-third of the world's useable supply of fresh water. And, while once upon a time this vast territory was looked upon as not much more than a huge, freezer-vault for the fur-hungry Hudson's Bay Company, today's adventurers come for riches of another kind. Here, within the frozen boundaries of this still largely unexplored land, is 13 percent of Canada's gold, more than 20 percent of its silver, over 40 percent of its land, one hundred percent of its tungsten, and vast, untapped resources of uranium, gas, and oil.

Within this expanse, three giant mountain ranges dominate the land: the Mackenzie Mountains along the Yukon border, the towering, craggy peaks of northern Baffin and Ellesmere Islands, and, at the southern end of Baffin Island, another range – actually part of the ancient Appalachian Range.

East of the Mackenzie District, the best known and most travelled area of the Northwest Territories, the terrain changes dramatically as the tree line dips southward. Here one leaves behind the forested lushness of the Mackenzie River valley, and the busy, frontier lifestyle of Yellowknife, Fort Smith, and Fort Simpson. Here the northern, horseshoe loop of the Canadian

(Precambrian) Shield adds a moonscape texture to the land. Formed more than 600 million years ago, the Canadian Shield is this country's geological core.

If the Districts of Keewatin and Franklin stand for anything in the Canadian psyche, they represent the land of the Inuit, a vast, lonely stretch of country – frozen and buried under snow for much of the year. On maps of the world it is this giant sweep of arctic islands toward the North Pole that gives Canada its claim to being the second largest country in the world.

In small arctic communities like Eskimo Point, Baker Lake, Rankin Inlet, Chesterfield Inlet, Igloolik, Spence Bay, Arctic Bay, Cambridge Bay, Pangnirtung, and Resolute, live a people whose ancestors have been traced to Siberia, whence it is thought that they came across the ice of Bering Strait.

For months on end the land is frozen, and despite the maps that celebrate its maze of lakes, rivers, and streams lying in all directions, they are not to be seen beneath the cover of ice and snow. What are to be seen are the huge ice floes where polar bears hunt for seals in temperatures that plunge to 40, 50, even 60 degrees below zero.

There are no trees here, but during the brief burst of arctic summer these giant tundra plains north and east of Hudson Bay come alive with millions of wildflowers. And myriads of birds – some seventy-five different species – make their annual visit to build their nests, hatch their young, and raise them. Herds of up to 100,000 caribou graze the tundra as they make they way toward their summer feeding grounds. In summer the rivers and streams are rich with arctic char and grayling, the lakes with trout, walleye, and great northern pike. Flocks of ducks, Canada geese, and other waterfowl darken the skies. And the north, albeit briefly, is very much alive.

The waters surrounding Canada's arctic islands are rich with marine life. Whales, beluga, narwhals, seals, and walrus feed here.

In the not so distant past, it is said that the Inuit word for tourism translated literally as "sports fishing." Today, although the numbers are still small, many Inuit villages are attracting other types of summer visitors – naturalists, photographers, artists, or those who have simply felt the lure of the north, and come to experience it firsthand.

Not oblivious to the appeal of its arctic frontier, the Canadian government has established Auyuittuq, the most northerly national park in the world. Its 8,290 square miles (21,470 sq. km.) on Baffin Island straddle the Arctic Circle and, as testament to the distance people will travel for a holiday adventure like none other, it is visited annually by more than 11,000 people. Mountains in Auyuittuq rise 7000 feet above sea level, their peaks crested by the Penny Ice Cap, 2200 square miles of ancient ice left over from the last Ice Age. The coastline of the park faces Davis Strait and is ragged with great fjords and cliffs of up to 3000 feet. It is on Baffin Island that birdwatchers will boast of having seen the gyrfalcon – seldom, if ever, found south of the Arctic Circle.

South of Auyuittuq, tucked into the southern tip of Baffin

Island, sits Frobisher Bay, the government and economic centre of the eastern Arctic. From this bustling town, a plane ride over some of the most spectacular landscape in the world can take you to Resolute, where signs at the airport warn the southern visitor not to feed the polar bears that – like racoons in southern cities – have come to expect castoff foods wherever people gather. In Resolute, the most northerly town on this continent, close to 200 people eat, sleep, work, or go to school where the sun never shines for at least three months during the winter, and summers bring three months of continuous daylight.

The northland is changing, and as it does, the southern visitor's image of the Canadian Arctic has all but disappeared.

Igloos were long ago replaced by tidy housing developments. And while dog teams are still owned by a few trappers and hunters, for the most part their excited yapping and barking has been replaced by the roar and drone of snowmobiles. The comings and goings of small aircraft are commonplace, and the frozen silence of the Arctic is alive now with the sounds of southern technology, as mining and drilling companies learn and test new ways to capture the vast riches that have long been impossible to reach beneath the arctic land and sea.

And yet, despite the increasing encroachment of the resource-hungry world, it is to the credit of the original inhabitants that the cultural bridge between past and future generations is being carefully built. Elders in every village still teach the art of living with the land. Young Inuit children study the wonders of science and space as brought to them by satellite and television; they also learn the techniques and skills with which their ancestors have lived at one with nature for centuries. History and mathematics are taught in government-run schools, while on the land young people learn to make clothing from the hides of caribou, and how to build snow houses in which to wait out storms while on the hunt or while tending trap lines. Inuit children watch the antics of puppets and cartoon characters of weekend television fare, while learning the songs and legends of a history of their own.

It is, say some visitors, as if the people of this vast region have an instinct for survival that sees beyond the move to take non-renewable resources from the north; that sees a day when once again the land will be given back to "the people," as they have always called themselves, and the people will return to living off the land.

Here in the icy waters of Hudson Bay, and north among the arctic islands, young Inuit men hunt whales with rifles from power-driven fishing boats, while learning from their fathers how to build kayaks of sealskin, and to fashion harpoons, and fishhooks of bone.

Here, near the Arctic Circle, young men who have left the traditional life of their villages to work on drilling platforms and operate earth-moving machinery in mines still track the seasonal movement of animals, understand the meaning of wolf howls, and know how to spot white ptarmigan and arctic hares on whiter snow.

The north is ever-changing, while remaining inexorably, magnificently the same.

THE PRAIRIE PROVINCES: ALBERTA, SASKATCHEWAN AND MANITOBA

To travel "from sea to sea" in Canada, from the rocky eastern shores of Newfoundland to the sand dune beaches on the western coast of Vancouver Island, the explorer must cross another "sea" – a 1000-mile, three-province-wide expanse that Canadians call their Prairie Provinces. And yet, to journey across Manitoba, Saskatchewan, and Alberta is to quickly abandon whatever mental images "the prairies" brings to mind. Here, as the name suggests, are indeed the country's wide-open spaces, yet somehow wider, more open than a first-time traveller could ever possibly dream. Yes, there are oceans of golden wheat, but incredibly vast oceans, stretching in all directions as far as the eye can see, more spectacularly golden than any visitor could possibly anticipate. And while the incredible history and immensity of this nation's wheatland has earned it the right to give Manitoba, Saskatchewan, and Alberta a common name, to the surprise of many (including many Canadians), fully less than one-third of the area of Canada's prairie tryptich of provinces can actually be described as prairie land. The rest is a country of spectacular contrasts on all sides – of lakes and waterways, of muskeg swamp, of grassland pastures for some of the largest cattle ranches in North America, of huge tracts of timber, and mile upon mile of rounded granite mounds where nothing grows.

In Alberta, the foothills roll away to the west, and the Canadian Rockies, which separate the province from British Columbia, jut their snow-capped peaks into the sky. In Manitoba, Lake Winnipeg, Lake Winnipegosis, and Lake Dauphin make the province one of the world's largest producers of freshwater fish: 36 million pounds a year, of which some 90 percent is exported to the United States. Of this 36 million-pound catch, one fish – the Winnipeg Goldeye – has made a fantastically successful leap onto breakfast, lunch, and dinner plates at fine hotels around the world.

In Saskatchewan, more than 70,000 farms grow the golden wheat and yellow rape that are Canada's two largest food crops, while the land itself holds one of the world's largest and richest supplies of potash, the key ingredient in fertilizers for farm states and countries around the world.

In Saskatchewan, it is not entirely surprising to find desert-like sand dunes of immense proportion surrounding the southern shores of Lake Athabaska, one of the 10 largest fresh-water lakes in the world. And yet one cannot help but express surprise at the fact that the province's southwestern Cypress Hills boast the same altitude as the highgrounds of Banff, Alberta.

Of the three provinces, Manitoba, with over 400 miles of Hudson Bay coastline, boasts the prairies' only ocean port, high on the coast of the Bay's northwestern shore.

In the Alberta Badlands surrounding Drumheller, weird caverns and hoodoos add a strange, eroded texture to the land, and tourists flock to the area to view recently unearthed dinosaur skeletons and bones.

The province of Manitoba, brought into Confederation as Canada's fifth province in 1870, is strongly linked in its history to the history of the Hudson's Bay Company, which contributed to the subsequent waves of immigration that have made the province one of the most multicultural in the Canadian firmament. It was here, in 1812, following years of struggle for control between the Hudson's Bay Company and the North West Company, that Lord Selkirk was granted vast tracts of land at the junction of the Red and Assiniboine Rivers, the site of present-day Winnipeg. It was here, as well, that the years of struggle between the British traders of the Bay and the Métis supporters of the once French-controlled North West Company continued, even after the rivals had joined forces in 1821. And it was in this fur-rich belt of the Canadian west that Louis Riel challenged the Canadian Government's surveyors with the words "This far and no farther," and provoked the years of struggle that culminated in the Rebellion of 1885.

It was in Manitoba's Red River Valley that early settlers first planted the grains that have made the Canadian prairies one of the greatest "breadbaskets" in the world. And it was grain that also brought to the province people from around the world, people of many cultures and backgrounds who truly saw a future in this promised land.

The province fulfilled that promise. The people stayed. And throughout Manitoba, place names salute the lands that made this province strong. Boissevain, Portage La Prairie, Ile des Chénes, and Aubigny reflect the enormous contribution to this province by the French. German Mennonites established the towns of Steinbach, Blumenort, and Altona. Settlers from Iceland built towns called Gimli, Reykyavik, and Lundar. The Scots founded Selkirk, Glencairn, and Clanwilliam. Dauphin, though French named, is widely recognized as the Ukrainian capital of Canada.

Alberta and Saskatchewan, on the other hand, did not join Canada as its eighth and ninth provinces until 1905, predated by Canada's first formal curling match at the Winnipeg Curling Club some 29 years earlier. By 1905, the University of Manitoba was welcoming its 28th freshman class.

It was Henry Hudson, on his fourth attempt at finding the Northwest Passage, who became the first European to sail into the magnificent inland sea which bears his name. Two years later, searching for some sign of Hudson's expedition, and unaware that the English explorer had been left to perish on the open water by mutineers, Sir Thomas Button sailed into the same body of water, reached the mouth of the Nelson River in 1612, and thus became the first white man to land in what is now Manitoba.

In 1619, Jens Munck landed a Danish party at the mouth of the Churchill River. But despite the discovery of this sailing route into the heart of the fur-rich Canadian interior, it was the overland and inland waterways routes mapped by Pierre Radisson and Chouart des Groseilliers that had the greatest impact on the opening of the prairie wilderness to the rest of the world. The most legendary of the *coureurs des bois*, it was these two French adventurers

who sailed out of Quebec City in the 1650s and returned two years later with 50 canoe-loads of valuable furs and news from the Indians with whom they had been trading of a country to the north and west that was rich beyond belief. If the fur country to the north, around the rim of Hudson Bay, was the best this new land had to offer, and the Bay offered more direct access to Europe, the trading possibilities were immense.

Unable to impress the French government with the importance and potential of their discovey and their dream, Radisson and his brother-in-law turned to Charles II of England. On May 2, 1670, Charles II signed the charter for "The Governor and Company of Adventurers of England Trading into Hudson's Bay," the forerunner of the Hudson's Bay Company.

Thus the new land was uncovered and explored; the wealth of the interior, not only in terms of furs, but also in terms of arable land, was described in wondrous detail, and immigrants and settlers began the westward trek into the Canadian west.

The rest is history.

Today in Alberta, the cities of Calgary and Edmonton (the provincial capital) boast populations of over 700,000 each. Forty-eight thousand people make their homes in Red Deer, while in the southern reaches of the province the cities of Lethbridge and Medicine Hat have populations of 56,000 and 40,000 respectively. Regina, Saskatchewan's capital, is also that province's largest city, followed by Saskatoon with a metropolitan population in excess of 165,000 people. By 1870, 12,000 settlers had arrived in the Red River settlement now known as Winnipeg. A century later, more than 600,000 people live there.

Today, of course, wheat and wildlife are still important factors in the economy of the Canadian west, but the lands of Saskatchewan, Manitoba, and Alberta have also been good in other ways.

The discovery of oil in Turner Valley, Alberta in 1912 was, for that province, the merest hint of things to come. It was a sign, the first significant strike in the British Empire, a reason for geologists to probe and prod the earth for 35 more years until, with the February, 1947, discovery of the Leduc oilfields south of Edmonton, Albertans could joyously announce that they had seen the future, and it was gloriously black.

Today, more that 12,000 oil wells are spread throughout the province, 2000 of them within 25 miles of Edmonton. More than 500 oil and gas exploration companies operate out of Calgary, the "Dallas of the north." At present, Alberta supplies more than eighty percent of Canada's oil, while geologists consider the mysteries of the province's northwestern corner where an estimated 900 billion additional barrels lie trapped in the Athabaska Tar Sands.

But the land in Alberta doesn't have to be drilled or mined and tunnelled to make it rich. It is in Alberta, at least if you are travelling east to west, that the Canadian Rockies loom above the surface of the prairie floor majestic, monumental, accessible to all. And while British Columbians will tell you that this mountainous backbone of the country jumps out of the Pacific Ocean, Albertans will convince you with their western charm that the Rockies truly begin where the prairies celebrate the completion of their westward sweep. It is said that some 21,000,000 visits are made to Canada's national parks every year, and the fact that Banff and Jasper National Parks attract the large majority of these visitors should come as no surprise.

Banff was chosen as the site for Canada's first national park more than 100 years ago. From its original 10 square miles, this jewel in the country's parks system has grown to more than 2500 square miles – one quarter the size of the Netherlands – and is widely regarded as one of the scenic wonders of the world. At Banff, the exceptionally beautiful Lake Louise sits jewel-like, cradled by snow-topped Rocky Mountain peaks, its blue-green waters coloured by the glacial silt and rock dust in the waters of Victoria Glacier.

Just north of Banff is Jasper, one of the most accessible parks in Canada, where more than 4200 square miles of mountain and wilderness preserve provide unlimited adventure and activity for the traveller-tourist. Here holidayers can take the sky-tram to the top of Whistler Mountain for lunch in the clouds, play 18 holes of golf, or take a therapeutic dip in the hot sulphur springs at Miette. The Icefield Highway between Banff and Jasper is one of the most scenic in Canada – 140 miles that encompass many spectacular views of the 3000-foot-thick Columbia Icefield.

In Alberta as well is the truly distinctive (including both Rocky Mountains and prairie grasslands) Waterton Lakes National Park; in combination with Glacier National Park, in Montana, it forms Waterton-Glacier International Peace Park, the first of its kind in the world. In the north, Alberta shares the 17,300 square miles of Wood Buffalo National Park with the Northwest Territories.

In Alberta, the tourist can also visit the province's Badlands, near Red Deer, where for many centuries the forces of nature have been busily shaping the canyons, strange stone pillars, and rock formations on a land once tropical and roamed by dinosaurs. For a better glimpse of things the way they used to be, the visitor should not miss a tour of Dinosaur Provincial Park in nearby Drumheller.

Alberta is also cattle country, its grasslands – particularly those in the foothills country of the southwest – providing some of the finest pasture land in Canada. And to celebrate the role that cattle, ranchers, and cowboys have played in the development of the province over the years, Albertans, every July, throw the *rootin'est, tootin'est,* party in the land. It's called the Calgary Stampede, and it turns that city on its ear. It's described in tourist brochures as the "Greatest Dad-Burned Outdoor Show on Earth," and it just might be. During the stampede, cowboys from all over Canada and the United States compete for rodeo prizes worth more than a quarter-of-a-million dollars in such daredevil pursuits as chuckwagon races, wrestling, bulldogging, bronc riding, calf and steer roping, Brahma bull and buffalo riding, wild horse races, and a bit of fun besides.

Not to be out-roped, out-rid, or out-done, the city of Edmonton celebrates its own history – one closely tied to the gold rush – with a July show of its own. Few places in Canada can match the spirit this city throws into Klondike Days, a ten-day festival that celebrates the time when Edmonton was one of the major stepping-off points for prospectors on their way to the gold-rush territory of the Yukon. Appropriately enough, the gold-rush legacy lingers on in both these cities.

As opposed to eastern style and the stern philosophy declaring that money belongs in banks, here in true western style, perhaps as though it were going out of style, money is well and truly spent. If Alberta's oil, natural gas, coal, and cattle wealth is visible anywhere, it is in Calgary and Edmonton, where already-modern skylines seem to grow more modern by the week, if not the day. Here ranchers spend like petro-kings, and workers from oil drilling sites dress like rodeo cowboys, from their $200 stetsons right on down to their $600 snakeskin boots.

Approaching either city, the visitor's first impression is of newness, projected by the geometry of real estate development – shining glass, marble, and steel building blocks that look as though they had been dropped onto the Alberta flatness overnight. And while much is indeed new in Calgary and Edmonton, one only has to meet the people who live in either, or wander the treed river-bank parks which both cities boast, or stop for lunch on a bustling downtown street to sense the warmth and good old-fashioned hospitality that westerners like to brag about.

In Calgary, at the junction of the Bow and Elbow Rivers, the skyline is dominated by the Calgary Tower which reaches a height of 620 feet. From the restaurant or the revolving observation deck at the top, one can look down on the city in all directions. Farther off, the view of the Alberta foothills and the Rocky Mountains is truly breathtaking.

On a more mundane level, the city has also won fame as the home of the Calgary *Stampeders* of the Canadian Football League.

The most northern of Canada's major cities is Edmonton, a full 350 miles north of the Canada-United States border, at the meeting point of the North Saskatchewan and Sturgeon Rivers. To truly feel the "pace" of western living, take a noonday stroll along Jasper Avenue. If sport is your idea of a day or a night on the town, the city is home base to the Stanley Cup winning hockey team – the Edmonton *Oilers* – and to the Canadian Football League's *Eskimos*.

The spirited rivalry between the cities of Edmonton and Calgary is legendary, extending far beyond the scheduling of Klondike Days to follow directly on the heels of the Calgary Stampede. If Calgary has a Planetarium (and it does) you can rest assured that Edmonton will have a Space Science Centre *and* an Aviation Hall of Fame. It does. When Edmonton built its magnificent Provincial Museum to celebrate Canada's 1967 Centennial, Calgary's equally grand Glenbow Provincial Museum and Art Gallery soon followed.

Calgary boasts the Inglewood Bird Sanctuary and a Dinosaur Park and Zoo. Edmonton is home to the Valley Zoo and the Muttart Conservatory, an imaginative botanical garden housed within five glass pyramids, each duplicating a different climate.

Spirited rivalry indeed! The same kind of spirit, say the citizens of both cities, that opened up the Canadian West.

With its great national and provincial parks system, the province of Alberta is a wildlife photographer's delight. Mountain goats and bighorn sheep roam the alpine meadows on the slopes of the mountains. In the forests and the lake country, elk, mule deer, moose, beaver and muskrat are plentiful.

The bears of Banff and Jasper are among those parks' most photographed inhabitants. This is *their* land and they wander the roads and trails of the parks so oblivious to the tourist crowds, and seemingly so tame, that park wardens spend a good deal of their time reminding visitors that they are indeed wild animals.

Though home to less than ten percent of Canada's population, the province of Saskatchewan produces more than sixty percent of the country's wheat crops, fifty percent of its rapeseed, and some forty-five percent of the country's flax. Oats, barley, and rye crops are abundant beyond belief. But as if the golden oceans of grain that sweep for miles across its tabletop landscape were somehow not enough, the Canadian prairies and the soil beneath them continue to surprise the people of Saskatchewan with riches that stagger the imagination.

Like Manitoba to the east, more than one third of Saskatchewan lies within the Canadian Shield, that vast Pre-Cambrian rocky swath that covers nearly 50 percent of Canada, and that holds deep beneath its granite surface much of this country's incredible and seemingly endless mineral wealth.

It was here, in the 1950s, while searching for oil, that prospectors stumbled on the world's largest and richest strata of potash – the rich and essential ingredient of fertilizers used throughout the agricultural world. Uranium, copper, and zinc are mined here, and the province is the only commercial source of helium in the country.

Like Alberta to the west, Saskatchewan is rich in oil and gas – second only to Alberta, in fact, in the production and supply of these fossil fuels. Because of them, new shapes have joined the familiar sight of giant grain harvesters sweeping through luxuriant golden plains of wheat. And today there are parts of the province where, as far as the eye can see, oil pumps dot the landscape harvesting black gold from under the prairie floor.

But the land rewards us in other ways as well and, like the provinces on either side of it, offers the visitor visual thrills beyond the plains that have made this part of Canada famous.

In Prince Albert National Park, a preserve of almost 1500 square miles near the geographical centre of the province, visitors can step into the cabin where the celebrated conservationist Grey Owl lived his final years, and stop at his grave nearby. The park is also the nesting ground and home to one of Canada's largest white pelican colonies.

In the southwestern corner are the province's legendary Cyprus Hills where tropical vegetation suggests that this area of Canada was once as warm as lands near the equator today. The provincial park here offers exciting walking and riding trails. There are fossil beds to explore, and wildlife such as antelope, moose, elk, and wild turkeys at almost every bend in the road.

The northern reaches of Saskatchewan are abundantly marked with rivers and literally thousands of lakes, and sportsfishermen from many parts of Canada and the United States visit every summer to try their luck in this richly forested end of the province. An estimated 20 billion tons of potash, enough to satisfy world demand for the next thousand years, is one thing, but in Saskatchewan it is also possible to fish a different lake every day for years on end. For many, that's a more impressive claim to fame.

At Methy Lake, in the northwest corner of the province, the historic Churchill River begins its 1000-mile journey across the tops of Saskatchewan and Manitoba toward the icy waters of Hudson Bay. The swift waters of the North and South Saskatchewan Rivers flow eastward across the province, converging at Saskatoon before continuing eastward where they empty into Lake Winnipeg.

Some 200 of northern Saskatchewan's lakes are fished commercially for pike, walleye, and whitefish.

Peculiar to the province's landscape are hundreds of thousands of granite "potholes" carved out by glaciers. Many fill with rain, or are fed by groundwater rich in minerals. As agents of nature they are an invaluable resource, promoting lush vegetation wherever they occur.

Canada's three prairie provinces lie within the northern reaches of the Mississippi and Central flyways, those north-south corridors followed by millions of song birds, game birds, and waterfowl that migrate during the spring and fall. And thus, in one more way, nature blesses Saskatchewan – by filling her parks and forested lake country with sights and sounds of infinite variety and delight.

Regina was named the capital of Saskatchewan when the province joined Confederation in 1905. Originally called "Pile o' Bones" by the Indians who piled the area with the bones of Buffalo as an offering to the hunt, this modern prairie city is built around Wascana Park, 2500 acres of sculptured, beautifully kept greenery surrounding a man-made lake. The elegant Saskatchewan Legislature Building, surrounded by fountains and formal gardens, and the University of Regina Campus, are both located here.

It is in Regina, that 1000 new recruits come annually to train in investigative techniques and law enforcement at the Royal Canadian Mounted Police training centre. In

November, Regina hosts the Canadian Western Exhibition, one of the largest agricultural fairs in the world. In August, the city taps its historical roots for ten days of horse racing and grandstand entertainment known as Buffalo Days. Canadian football fans need no reminding that the city is also home to the Saskatchewan *Roughriders*.

"The City of Bridges," as Saskatoon is called, for the six spans that cross the South Saskatchewan River here, is the second largest city in the province. And here, during the week-long hoopla of the city's July Pioneer Days celebration, local wags love to tell the story of how the city was founded in 1883 by whiskey-hating zealots from eastern Canada, heaven-bent on creating a teetotaller's paradise far from the corrupting influences of civilization. Twenty years later, the story goes, the population had swelled to 113.

At Saskatoon, a 5.5 million-bushel grain elevator attests to the city's involvement in the production of wheat. The University of Saskatchewan, where in 1952 Cobalt-60 was first used in the treatment of cancer, is located here. So is the highest man-made mountain in Canada, a 300-foot slope created for skiing events in the 1971 Canadian Winter Games, and still in use today.

It is sometimes said that the origins of the multi-cultural Canada we know today are firmly rooted in the Manitoba soil, and even if that statement were only partly true, Canada would owe a debt of gratitude to this most easterly of its prairie provinces as large as the land itself. No other province has benefited from the rich diversity of culture and skills from other lands as much as this one has. And for that reason alone no other province has been as adept at passing those benefits along.

The history of Manitoba tells it all.

Here is a province that Canadians can claim was settled by the world. For in the waves of immigration that followed the original fur traders of England and France, people from many nations, and from many walks of life, left their homes to build new ones in a country that promised the reality of dreams.

Scots, Irish, English came. Swedes, Austrians, Germans, and Galicians. Russians, French, Jews, Ukrainians, Icelanders, Americans, and Poles arrived, convinced that the hardship of getting here, in many cases with families, would be amply rewarded by a country that was said to be rich not only on the land, but also in its lakes and rivers and in the ocean waters on its northern shore. For many, a new start in an uninhabited, unexplored, and unsettled territory – said to be frozen and under snow for up to seven months of the year – was exactly what they had been waiting for. And despite the years of hardship which we know they endured, history proved them right.

The pattern has continued to the present day and helps explain the delight of visitors to Winnipeg who, when planning a dinner and night on the town, discover a restaurant guide that tells them they have a choice of American, Austrian, Chinese, Danish, East Indian, English, French, German, Greek, Hungarian, Italian, Japanese, Caribbean, Swiss, Mexican, Chilean, Yugoslavian, Russian, Jewish, Polish, Ukrainian, *or* Canadian food, to name a few.

For most Canadians, Winnipeg, or more specifically the intersection of Portage Avenue and Main Street, is where the west begins. Curiously, this famous intersection is within a stone's throw of where the Canadian west actually did begin. For it was at the intersection of the Red and Assiniboine Rivers, a few modern city blocks away, in fact, that the famous French explorer Pierre de La Vérendrye built Fort Rouge in 1738. It was here he traded with the Indians for the rich pelts from the northern forests. It is here, today, to what has grown to become Canada's fourth largest city, that auctions still attract wealthy fur buyers from around the world.

The Red River Valley that all but broke the spirit of the Scots brought here by Lord Selkirk in the early 1800s is now home to more than 650,000 people from across the globe.

Here, despite the fierce conflicts of interest that precipitated the Riel Rebellion, a life-size statue of Louis Riel – the Métis leader hanged for treason in 1885 – stands in a place of honour near the Manitoba Legislature Building in downtown Winnipeg. On the rooftop spire of that same building is Winnipeg's famous Golden Boy, a gilded statue of a running youth said to symbolize progress and development throughout Manitoba.

In Manitoba, progress and development are everywhere. Brandon, the province's second largest city, is Manitoba's chief grain-shipping centre, and is frequently referred to as The Wheat City of Canada. Here, on the banks of the Assiniboine River, stately mansions tell of the riches the city has enjoyed, while word from the Grain Exchange (now called the Winnipeg Commodities Exchange) speaks of wealth to come.

In the northland, the pioneer spirit which built this province lives on. At Flin Flon, Thompson, and The Pas, it is alive and well in the mining, lumbering, and trapping interests of the region.

Portage la Prairie – on the banks of the Assiniboine, and the site of some of the province's richest vegetable farms – was originally called Fort la Reine. Like Winnipeg before it, it too was originally one of the many fur-trading centres established by Pierre de La Vérendrye and his sons as they pushed across the prairies toward the Canadian Rockies in the west.

Situated on the east bank of the Red River, directly across from Winnipeg, is St. Boniface – the largest French-speaking city in Canada outside the province of Quebec. There is a monument to La Vérendrye here and, nearby, visitors can visit the grave of Louis Riel in the churchyard of the St. Boniface Basilica.

The settlers who blessed Manitoba with the cultural heritage of much of Europe would be proud of their province's capital today, for in this relatively small city, by North American standards, an artistic and cultural community thrives that is known and envied throughout the world. Six professional performing arts companies exist here that regularly present everything from drama

by the Spirit, a 1913 steam locomotive which now serves as the tourist bureau.

Within a few minutes walk, the visitor can admire the splendor of pre-Confederation limestone buildings, restored 19th century dockyards, museums and one of the most scenic and busy waterfronts in the province. There's also Fort Henry, the great fortress that overlooks the city.

Boat tours clog the harbor and on any given day during the season you can see yachts and cruisers from all around the Great Lakes and New York. You can also see Royal Military College with its groomed lawns and reputation as Canada's most up-to-date training facility.

Most of the yachts travelling up and down the Great Lakes call the Golden Horseshoe – the wide swing of land south and west of Toronto – their home port.

Hamilton, with most of Ontario's steel production including the huge Stelco, has one of the finer harbors in the province and the horseshoe swings along the lake through the wine country districts around St. Catherines to historic Niagara-on-the-Lake, home of the Shaw festival, and Niagara Falls itself.

Slightly north in the escarpment area is Festival Country where Stratford holds court with its annual Shakespearean festival. But there's much more than the famous summer theatre.

There's the covered bridge at West Montrose, the Farmer's Market at Kitchener, Mennonite country, the Tooth of Time Gorge at Elora, miles of sandy beaches and the shops and local foods of Elmira, Elora and Guelph.

In Rockton, there's the famous African Lion Safari and if you haven't seen a lion or a tiger recently, you can drive your car through the park and see hundreds of animals running loose.

Nearby are several excellent parks and picnic areas or you can just drive the few miles to Niagara Falls and look at one of the world's great attractions.

High above the Niagara Gorge is the Spanish Aero Car which is a must-in-a-lifetime ride for many. There is also an ancient legend at the falls about a beautiful princess named Lelawala who went over them in a white birch-bark canoe to appease the gods. She died in the falls, but it is said that her ghost lives on in the caves below the cataract, caves you can see from the sturdy little cruise ships called *Maid of the Mist.*

Hungry? Don't miss Kitchener and its neighboring city of Waterloo with their famous farmers' markets. You can buy everything from fresh produce to the finest fruit in Ontario and wonderful Mennonite pies and sausage. Kitchener is also home to Oktoberfest, Canada's largest fall festival of beer, beer and more beer.

Stratford is only an hour away by car from Kitchener but the festival is so popular that many performances are sold out months in advance. Among the main attractions of the lovely little centre are its magnificent parks, hardby the theatre with swans, ducks and some of the finest picnic areas in Ontario.

Or if the beach is more to your liking, Ontario offers the famous Grand Bend, miles and miles of soft sand and balmy Lake Huron water. You can picnic there or drive to nearby Blyth for its summer festival.

London, the unofficial capital of southwestern Ontario, is also close by, with its annual fair, the huge Western University and some of the finest cattle and agricultural land in the province.

If you're there in the fall, don't miss Western Fair, a true taste of all that is good in southwestern Ontario – rides, agricultural exhibits, horses, cattle sheep and hogs. There's also Storybook Gardens for the children.

Hamilton, besides its booming industrial base, is one of the prettier areas of the Horseshoe with its mountain, the famous botanical gardens and Dundurn Castle where the tiles were made by the Minton China people.

And, further down the 401 Highway, the official road of southern Ontario, is Windsor which shares an international bridge and tunnel with Detroit. It, with Oshawa and Oakville, also shares honors as Canada's automotive capital.

Windsor also shares a spectacular yearly International Freedom Festival with Detroit along the river where they claim more fireworks are shot off than in any other place in the world.

The city itself has a beautifully-renovated downtown shopping area and miles of wonderful park along the Detroit River. And when was the last time you had lunch and dinner in two separate countries only a minute apart?

Along Lake Huron to the north and up to Georgian Bay are some of Ontario's finest cottage and beach areas, attracting yearly renters from deep in the U.S. The creme-de-la-creme area is still the Muskokas, however, where million dollar country homes sit on their own private islands.

And some of Ontario's finest fishing is in the Kawartha lakes district, just north of Peterborough and Kindsay. Or, you can rough it in huge Algonquin Park where wildlife is wildlife, 2,910 square miles of wilderness, lakes and hardwood forest. There are ten nature trails with breathtaking views from Lookout Trail or around Smoke and Tea Lakes.

Or try the Haliburtons with its famous Skyline Park and great outcropping of Precambrian Shield, offering spectacular views and scenery.

The North is Ontario's best kept secret and is much more than huge pulp mills, mines and scrub land.

Start to the North by taking The Big Canoe, the name of the ferry that goes from Tobermory across Georgian Bay to Manitoulin Island, the largest fresh water island in the world.

If you don't mind climbing, you can get a spectacular view of the island by driving to Meldrum Lake (population 45) and go up to the top of the Mississaugi Lighthouse, the exact point where the explorer LaSalle wrecked his ship, the *Griffin*.

Gore Bay on the island is also popular with the nearby Bridal Veil Falls. But if you want to see something different, drop in at the Gore Bay jail where the cells have been converted into display rooms for a museum.

The island has a causeway at Little Current which nicely leads you into Northern Ontario proper and at night you can watch the spectacular sights of molten slag pouring from the many nickel mines.

The capital of the North is Sudbury, home of the huge nickel mines of Inco Ltd. The city, with a population of 100,000, is full of beautiful parks and lakes, plus wonderful boating and swimming and museums. It is also the home of the new Science Centre North, a stunning provincial attraction that offers hours and hours of fun.

If you want to visit a nickel mine, you can go into the Big Nickel, marked by a 30-foot high replica of the 1951 commemorative coin.

And, if you're a fisherman, Sudbury is the takeoff point for fly-in expeditions to literally thousands of unspoiled lakes full of speckled trout, lake trout, bass and pike.

French River, about an hour from Sudbury, runs 70 miles from Lake Nippissing to Georgian Bay and was the main canoe route for the famous Voyageurs in their travels from the Atlantic, down the St. Lawrence, around the Great Lakes and into Western Canada.

As early as 1620, French Canadians paddled their 40-foot freight canoes loaded with furs along this waterway and most of the famous explorers followed the route.

Nearby is Parry Sound, named to honor Arctic explorer Sir William Edward Parry. It is the main access point to the famous 30,000 Islands, each marked by a rock with a number.

Further south is the aforementioned Ste. Marie among the Hurons which was burned to the ground by the missionaries because of Indian Wars.

But now, after decades of archeological and historical research, the old mission stands today. More than 20 buildings have been carefully reconstructed as they were 350 years ago. The everyday life of the community is expertly brought to life by guides who welcome you and demonstrate the life of the 17th century.

Another interesting spot in the North is Sault Ste. Marie, a steel town with one of the most breath-taking tourist rides in Canada. It's called the Algoma Central Railway and for a small charge you can take an excursion into Agawa Canyon, the most beautiful area in Ontario for fall color.

It's all in Ontario, where the provincial government has

rightly come up with a slogan: Is there any other place you'd rather be?

QUEBEC

Quebec has it all.

From the north, with its huge hydro-electric developments, mines, lakes and natural resources to the south, with the cosmopolitan City of Montreal, the mighty St. Lawrence and historic Quebec City, this province of more than 7 million is a virtual celebration of Canada.

Historically, Quebec is a textbook of Canada 400 years ago and today, one can still imagine the brave little ships of the French explorers travelling up the St. Lawrence into the then-uncharted heartland of Canada.

And, if Quebec has a pulsating heart, either English or French, it is Quebec City, the oldest continuously-inhabited settlement in North America and the capital of this mighty first settlement in the nation.

Originally, this wonderful city was the Indian village of Stadacona until it was visited by Jacques Cartier in his travels up the St. Lawrence, a tiny man in a tiny ship whose horizons were limited only by the depth under his keel.

If was founded for the French as a fur-trading post by Samuel de Champlain in 1608, another brave explorer who was convinced there was a great inland sea within this country where trees, beaver and fish proved the original prime resources.

But even without the first-imagined riches of gold, Quebec City offered much more and played a crucial role in the development of New France, serving as its capital and the conduit for shipment of beaver back to France.

Today, a visitor to the walled city high above the river can easily experience the rush of history with many buildings and houses dating back to those early days of Canada.

The British captured the city in 1759 and gained official possession in 1763 but they continued to maintain it as the political and military centre of Canada, capitalizing on the huge timber growth to make Quebec City the ship-building heart of Canada, a tradition that lingers today up and down the St. Lawrence and in the beautiful Saguenay area.

The city itself is breathtaking, situated at a narrowing of the river and dominated by the Upper Town on Cape Diamond and the Lower Town below its narrow cobbled streets and historic buildings.

The city is dominated by the famous Plains of Abraham where the British general Wolfe defeated the French Montcalm in 1759, in a battle that changed the course of Canadian history. Ironically, both generals died within hours of the conflict.

With a population of more than 480,000, Quebec is one

of Canada's top tourist attractions with some of the finest restaurants in the world, the historic Chateau Frontenac hotel, the National Assembly buildings, Artillery Park, Breakneck Stairs, Cartier-Brebuf Park, the Citadel itself, the Battlefields Park and the Walls and Gates.

And it is fitting that Quebec – with the of motto Don de Dieu Ferray Valoir (God's Gift To Make the Most) – has spent millions of dollars to restore its Lower Town, exactly as it looked three centuries ago in the days of Louis XIII, Champlain and Governor Frontenac.

Great care has been taken to rebuild the old houses of the early French regime until now this beautiful cradle of civilization for Canada looks like the colony of 1608, thanks to painstaking work of 20th-century historians, archeologists and architects.

The first restoration was Maison Chevalier in 1955 but the area really began to move in 1960 when the Historic Monuments Board approached the Quebec government with a detailed brief indentifying the historic buildings in the old quarter – an area, it must be noted, that contains some of the city's top restaurants and discos.

The Maison Chevalier, completely restored, is now a museum of early Quebec furniture and faces La Place Royale, the redevelopment that is far larger than the modest quadrangle where Champlain built his Habitation in 1608.

A bust of Louis XIV now stands beside the picturesque church of Notre-Dame-des-Victoires and the king overlooks the narrow streets that still carry their original names – Sous-le-Fort, Cul-de-Sac, Cote de la Montagne, du Porche and Notre Dame.

To date, almost 80 buildings and sites have been purchased and renovated and most have been named after the original owners. The rebuilt Maison Fornel, for example, houses the many objects found on the site from the smallest rusty nail to coins dating back to 1588.

The most important discovery in this most important area of Canada is the site of the Royal Battery, one of the earliest defence systems in North America. The cannon emplacement was built in 1691 to protect the town from attack but it was destroyed in 1760 and disappeared under later buildings.

You can tour the Old Town today with guides from the provincial government or you can take the ferry to Levis, across the St. Lawrence, and look up at Canada as it was known to the explorers, experiencing again the thrill that must have greeted Cartier and Champlain.

But Quebec City is much, much more than history. It is also one of Canada's happiest places, winter and summer, and famed for its annual week-long Winter Carnaval, a celebration first held in 1894.

It endures today with hundreds of thousands of visitors, rivalling the Mardi Gras as a pre-Lenten festival in late February and featuring Jean Bonhomme – also called Bonhomme Carnaval – the only talking snowman in the world.

For some, however, Quebec City is famous for its restaurants. It's said you can't get a bad meal or a bad wine and there's something for everyone, from the tiny bars, bistros and brasseries to the famous and celebrated grand rooms which may be housed in a historical building like La Poudriere, the old powder room.

Up the river from Quebec is Montreal, a city that never sleeps and an area, with a population of 2.7 million, that is the largest French-speaking city in Canada.

Cartier visited the area first when it was the Indian village of Hochelaga and named it Mont Royal after the mountain that dominates the area. It was settled in 1642 by Maisonneuve as the colony of Ville-Marie, a name that gave way to Montreal, even though many streets still carry derivations of the old name.

Like Quebec City down the river (Quebecois always say the St. Lawrence flows down to the ocean, never up to the Great Lakes of Ontario and the United States), Montreal's early growth was related to the fur trade but explorers quickly discovered it was on an axis near the Ottawa River, Richelieu and the Great Lakes, making it quickly the early boom town of Canada.

By the late 1700s, Montreal was the dominant city of North America in territorial influence and became the headquarters of the North West Company, Canada's first seaport and later, a railway terminus.

Today, it is happily bilingual (although French is much more prevalent than English) and rivals Toronto in Ontario as the principal commercial, financial and manufacturing centre of Canada. Distinctive for its two major cultural groups, French and English, the city has undergone a major transition in the last 20 years.

Now, there's the famous Place Ville Marie, an underground and high-rise shopping and entertainment centre that first introduced Canada to the wonders of underground living during the cold winter months.

The success of Place Ville Marie quickly spawned multi-functioned areas like Place Bonaventure and Place du Canada but Montreal really stunned the world when it staged EXPO 67, a World Fair that drew millions.

By then the city had also attracted Canada's first professional baseball team, the *Expos*, capitalized on one of the finest hockey teams in the world, the *Canadiens*, and won a dynasty of Grey Cups with the Canadian Football League *Alouettes* (now the Concorde), and had built one of the finest subway systems in the world. But the city and the province weren't finished.

In 1976, the eyes of the world turned again to Montreal for the Olympic Games, with thousands of reporters telling millions of people nightly about the historic city and its Old Section (where it is said you can still sing the songs of the coureurs de bois), Bonsecours Market, Chateau de Ramezay, Hotel Dieu, Man and His World (a continuation of Expo), Place des Arts and Place d'Armes.

Even without the tremendous publicity, Montreal had a major reputation across North America as the cultural heart of Quebec and a city with a warm welcome from the many fine hotels (it is one of the convention centres of Canada) to the restaurants, night spots and bars.

But no article on Quebec is complete without a reference to the proud Quebecois, the people of this great province who have long sought their own identity.

Did you know that when Quebec was part of the French North American Empire, its French-speaking settlers were known as the Canadiens, the same proud name that is now carried by Montreal's National Hockey League team?

In 1763 after the conquest of New France, the people became British subjects in a colony known as the province of Quebec. After the founding of the United Canada in 1841, even the British Americans called themselves Canadians.

That line continued until Confederation with the official province of Quebec in 1867, and the French-speaking identity of this great and historic area of Canada persevered until the 1950s when the French-speaking people of the province began to ask themselves if it would not be more realistic to promote their economic and cultural progress by establishing bilingualism in Canada.

Then, the Quebecois were born. Maurice Duplessis struggled to consolidate Quebec's autonomy and helped the Quebecois choose their own destiny, a course that flowed to Ottawa when the then prime minister, Louis Saint-Laurent, suddenly discovered, when he tried to influence his own people, that there was a Quiet Revolution in his province by the Great River.

That hunt for an identity was later joined by Jean Lesage, Rene Lesveque and others and the government of 1962 adopted a motto that Quebec should become "masters of our own house" – an important stepping stone on the road to a new set of rules, both for the province and Canada, which up until then ignored the French fact.

When the Union Nationale Party under the leadership of Daniel Johnson came back into power in 1966, it had no choice but to complete the reform policies first adopted by Lesage. Then, when the Parti Quebecois proposed a program to achieve this goal in 1970, voters flocked to the banner.

Now, the Parti Quebecois is pursuing an active role towards the future, protecting the French in Quebec and ensuring a bilingual participation in Canada.

But, politics aside, no story about Quebec is complete without a rundown of the natural wonders of the province, from the north shore coast of the Gaspé where world-famous wonders like Percé Rock provide one of the finest bird sanctuaries in North America to the unspoiled north shore of the St. Lawrence, a veritable feast of connected towns, villages and inns.

Time was, wealthy Americans used to look for tiny local attractions in Canada where pets, nurses and nannies were encouraged and welcomed far away from the madding crowds of big cities in the U.S. So they took themselves off to the Charlevoix area of Quebec along the peaceful shores of the great river.

Several built incredible summer palaces in the towns of La Malbaie, Pointe-au-Pic and Cap-à-l'Aigle, establishing some of the oldest summer resort areas in North America.

Today, the area is favored by prime ministers and kings and Pointe-au-Pic boasts the magnificent Manoir Richelieu, built in 1899 and then destroyed by fire and rebuilt in 1928.

The 305-room castle now belongs to the Quebec government, and is a summer resort offering golf and swimming, tennis, riding, fishing croquet and lawn bowling. It is also a favourite getaway for many Canadian politicians.

On the other side is Cap-à-l'Aigle, a community named by Champlain for the resting place of many eagles along the rock cape – eagles that still abound today.

Then there's the incredible skiing area of Le Massif about 80 kilometres north of Quebec City, a triple-peak formation of mountains that form a natural amphitheatre.

Several skiing experts put the area ahead of Banff's famous Mount Norquay because of the quality of the snow, which is powder perfect, they say. The reason is the humidity which rises from the river, a phenomenon weathermen call orographic precipitation.

The Quebec government began developing the peaks in the early 1970s, and spent $4 million buying land and cutting trails. Now the area is full of lifts and nearby inns which offer everything from hospitality to five-star gourmet dining. But the largest single concentration of ski areas in North America is the Laurentians, near Montreal, which offer an array of hospitable inns, fine food and nightlife that can easily stretch into the early morning.

The mountain areas, only minutes from Montreal by car, bus or train, boast 32 Alpine and 50 cross-country centers in a 40-mile span that starts at St. Sauver and extends to Mont Tremblant, the giant mountain of Eastern Canada.

In between, you'll find such centres as Piedmont, Mont-Gabriel, Ste. Adele, Ste. Agathe, Ste. Margaret, Val Morin and Val David, all accessible by train, or a highway which is called, appropriately, the Laurentian autoroute.

More than 200 lifts, including 25 chairlifts, carry skiers up hills ranging from a few hundred feet to Mont Tremblant's 2,200-foot vertical drop. There are expert runs, and others gentle enough for beginners and the inns and resorts offer virtually everything.

Ste. Adele, for example, pulsates with apres-ski revelry in famous night spots like La Louisiane, Bourbon Street, and discos such as Vaudeville and JTs. Gray Rocks, five miles past St. Jovite, is a magnet for singles, while the rugged but beautiful lodges boast outstanding dining room fare.

But man cannot live on skiing alone, which brings us to the famous area of the Eastern Townships across the river from Montreal and close to the American border. Sherbrooke is the unofficial capital of this area of Quebec, a quiet oasis in a tumultuous land that quite simply grew up differently.

It was settled by United Empire Loyalists fleeing the American Revolution and allowed to go its own way for more than a century while Montreal developed in the French fact just a few bridges to the north.

Now, the situation has changed, with most people having French as their first language. But it is still one of the most perfectly bilingual areas in Canada, a place where many natives speak either language without a trace of an accent.

The townships, known in French as Estrie, are equally well known by tourists who come from Ontario and northern New York state, luxuriating in the deep green hills, rolling farmland, family restaurants, roadside antique barns or summer theatres that offer outstanding fare in both French and English.

Mont Orford Park is a favorite camping area, and Magog is a resort town where you can hear the strains of a violin, flute or harp at the famous Orford Art Centre.

At St. Benoit-du-Lac, a massive Benedictine abbey, you can listen to Gregorian chants or buy cheese, chocolate and cider made by the Order. Family establishments are still a big hit in the region and many restaurants double as town bakeries.

The resort area of North Hatley is a prime example of the days when millionaires from Montreal and neighboring U.S. states built palatial cottages long before they discovered the dubious joys of jet-setting.

The zoo at Granby is also well-known because it makes up in quality and style for what it lacks in area. It packs its 89 acres with a display of animals from around the world, beautiful flower gardens, an overhead tram ride and carnivals for children.

Right across Rue Bourget from the zoo is one of the finest automobile museums in the country, containing long-forgotten brand names from the turn of the century. Most are in such condition that it's difficult to believe they were bought for as little as $25 from owners anxious to get rid of them.

Louis St. Laurent was born in the town of Compton and you can still see the original St. Laurent family grocery which the Quebec government is restoring to honor the late prime minister.

Sherbrooke itself is much, much more than a business and manufacturing centre. Its picturesque location and easy-going lifestyle make it a resort capital of the region where hello and bonjour translate simply as welcome.

Finally, you can feel Quebec through its natural beauty, history and attractions. The province is alive winter and summer, spring and fall with festivals and celebrations, either honoring cultural events or just having fun.

One prime example is Man and his World and the La Ronde amusement park on the site of Expo 67 in Montreal. It's a natural growth of Expo 67 and offers some of the finest international exhibitions in the country, everything from flowers to roller coasters.

In the Saguenay district, there's the annual July festival and Lac St. Jean marathon swim, an event not to be missed by anyone who loves water or the natural beauty of provincial parks. Or you can take a cruise ride up and down the river and experience again the same majesty, the same excitement that greeted the fur traders and voyageurs of New France hundreds of years ago.

And remember, Quebec City has just celebrated the 450th anniversary of the voyage of Jacques Cartier. He too would have been proud of the accomplishments, cultural and otherwise, of the new Quebec today.

It's really hard to believe it was that long ago because the province, through good times and bad, has proven itself as Canada's first and foremost. Don't believe us – just ask anyone, on either side of the river, in French or in English.

Quebec has, it must be said, la joie de vie, or for the English – the love of life.

THE ATLANTIC PROVINCES: NOVA SCOTIA, NEW BRUNSWICK, P.E.I. AND NEWFOUNDLAND

The four provinces of Atlantic Canada are studies in contrast and beauty. Nowhere in the country is there such a mix of sea and scenery, coastline and forests, people and agriculture, history and heritage.

From the fish and booming offshore oil industry of Newfoundland to the pulp and nuclear power of New Brunswick, from the natural gas and coal of Nova Scotia to the potatoes and beaches of Prince Edward Island, there's something for everyone in the East – the name all use to describe this stunning area of Canada.

Marked by warm summers and clement winters, Atlantic Canada has always been one of the favorite vacation spots for North America, drawing tourists from across the United States, Europe and the other six provinces, tourists who want uncrowded beaches, clean air and a hearty East Coast welcome.

But beneath the welcome there's much more to these sturdy provinces, dating back to the 1500s and settled by French, English and Loyalists, men and women who quickly learned that Atlantic Canada was the natural water entry to the rest of the Dominion.

Newfoundland, for example, the last province to join Confederation in 1949, has persevered through good times and bad, justly earning its nickname of the Rock. Now, it is pinning its hopes on a huge find of oil just off the

Grand Banks, a find that some say could provide Canada's energy needs for the foreseeable future.

But the Island province, marked by capital St. John's, the most easterly city in Canada, still counts on its billion dollar fishing industry as the mainstay of its economy.

Nova Scotia, with 1 million people the largest of the Atlantic provinces, is in a similar situation, but this time it's gas, not oil. Huge pools of natural gas have been discovered off Sable Island and the South Shore and test wells are being sunk.

However, the province with its proud symbol, the racing schooner *Bluenose*, makes its economy go with coal and steel from Cape Breton, agriculture and marvelous fruit from the Annapolis Valley and, of course, the fish and lobster of the South Shore, some of the best in the world.

And speaking of best, tiny Prince Edward Island, with only 110,000 people, and 110 miles long, tip to tip, raises the best potatoes in the world, famous everywhere. The Island also has a booming lobster and fishing industry, and its Malpeque oysters are prized on tables from New York to New Orleans.

New Brunswick, the forest province, has the pulp, the shipbuilding (an art that goes back generations, to when four-masted windjammers were built in Saint John) and the nuclear power plant. It also has the refining capabilities in Saint John to provide oil and gasoline to the rest of the East.

But the Atlantic Provinces really shine with tourism. It's one of the largest industries in P.E.I., Nova Scotia and New Brunswick and the Newfoundland government is quickly realizing the potential bonanza with a major infusion of new promotion funds.

Let's look now at these four beautiful provinces, areas of Canada so steeped in history and tradition that it's easy to linger and let their rugged natural beauty overwhelm you.

NEWFOUNDLAND

Imagine a postcard city and you've got St. John's, one of the oldest inhabited towns in North America, and the site of a marker placed in 1583 by Sir Humphrey Gilbert claiming possession of the Island for England.

The abundance of cod was the original lure to Newfoundland and St. John's and by 1801 the settlement had 3,420 people, quickly becoming the principal commercial judicial and administrative centre for Newfoundland.

Located hard by the Avalon Peninsula, the city is crammed with interesting sights and scenery. There's a strong Irish feeling in the area, with stony, moss-covered land and Cape Spear, the point of North America closest to Ireland.

The lighthouse at Cape Spear is a National Historic Park, serving from 1836, and the buildings have all been restored. Witless Bay is also nearby, and you can see the bird sanctuary of Gull Island, one of the world's largest

nesting areas for petrels, kittiwakes, puffins, murres and razorbills.

Further up the Peninsula, there's Ferryland where the British fought the French in a series of battles during the Seven Years War. And the area is marked by the graves of countless seamen who died in wrecks when ships went aground on treacherous reefs.

Cape St. Mary's is another top bird sanctuary, where the nesting colonies blanket a rock pillar which has split away from the mainland. West on the Peninsula is Placentia, where the French built their great capital in the mid-1600s, even though the British in St. John's claimed the whole island.

At first, Placentia was called Plaisance because of its harbor, fresh water and long, rocky beach, perfect for fish drying. But Britain got it back in the Treaty of Utrecht in 1713 and quickly anglicized it to its present name.

Only a few miles away is Argentia, where a summer-only ferry docks after an 18-hour one-way trip from Nova Scotia and where, in 1941 in the bay, President Franklin D. Roosevelt and Prime Minister Winston Churchill secretly met aboard *HMS Prince of Wales* to sign the Atlantic Charter.

The Peninsula is dotted with tiny towns and villages or outports with names like Heart's Content and Dildo, where whales frequently gather. But everything starts and ends in St. John's.

The city is known for its famous deep water harbor, and it's so small and compact that everywhere there is a good view. Painted clapboard houses still dot the harbor and the streets are tiered up from the waterside itself.

Signal Hill dominates the harbor entrance and the Anglican Cathedral is visible from anywhere downtown. Further outside the city (but nothing is far in St. John's) are the legislature buildings and huge Memorial University, the main upper learning centre for the province.

You can travel Newfoundland by car on the new TransCanada highway, and up near Corner Brook there's a sign warning of high winds, erected because the province's little rail line, once called the Newfie Bullet, actually employed a man in the area to warn of winds because they might blow the tiny train off the tracks.

It's an easy trip to Newfoundland across the Cabot Strait by ferry from Cape Breton, a boat ride that features a bar serving Newfie Screech, the mix of rum and molasses guaranteed to curl your hair.

The ferry docks at Port aux Basques, and there you pick up the Highway, a road marked by provincial parks all the 562 miles over to St. John's. One of the best is the Terra Nova Park on the Atlantic, which can take up to two days to visit.

Grand Falls is the island's third largest city behind St. John's and Cornerbrook and is known for pulp and paper and its fabulous salmon fishing. Down the Gander River is Gander, a town chosen as a World War II trans-Atlantic air base and still used as a refuelling stop.

The oldest community in the province is Salvage on Bonavista Bay and it was not even reachable by road until after the Second World War.

And, oh yes, Newfoundland also includes Labrador, that huge, rugged area north of Quebec that has one of the largest hydro-electric generating stations in Canada.

NOVA SCOTIA

This province is the sea. It is its lifeblood, heritage and future and it is fitting that its symbol is the *Bluenose*, the world's fastest racing schooner now immortalized on the Canadian dime.

A replica of the famous schooner, the *Bluenose II* is now berthed in Halifax at the Historic Properties on the waterfront, and the ship is an important part of the transformation of this historic city.

The capital of the province and the leading city in Atlantic Canada, Halifax was founded in 1749 as a fortified British settlement (it was called Chebucto by the Indians) and later settled by United Empire Loyalists.

It served for many years as a military garrison marked by the famous Citadel on the hill, but its superb deepwater harbor quickly drew more and more seafarers. The city grew in the 19th and 20th century into the predominant commercial and administrative centre for Nova Scotia and became a national port.

Today, it is headquarters of the Royal Canadian Navy and much of the labor force in Halifax and the neighboring city of Dartmouth across the harbor, is employed by the defence ministry.

The city had a black period, however, and was devastated by the Halifax Explosion in December, 1917, when the Norwegian freighter *Imo* collided with the French munitions ship, the *Mont Blanc*. The resulting explosion levelled the city and killed 2,000.

But the rebuilding has now produced one of the more beautiful capitals of Canada from the historic Citadel to the Historic Properties and Privateers Wharf. It is also the seat of the legislature and the home of Dalbousie University, the largest institution of its type in Atlantic Canada.

South of Halifax is the South Shore, one of the more beautiful areas of the country, known for picturesque fishing villages and vacation areas like Chester. Further down the coast is Lunenburg, where both Bluenoses were built, and the home of the Fisheries Museum, which includes a rum runner from Prohibition Days.

Peggy's Cove is Canada's most famous fishing village and is packed with tourists winter and summer. But there are dozens of other villages and hamlets where you could be the only visitor.

Gabarus on Cape Breton Island, joined to Mainland Nova Scotia by a causeway, is a good example, and others are Neil's Harbour and Bay St. Lawrence, both located on the picturesque Cabot Trail in northern Cape Breton.

The Trail itself is Atlantic Canada's best known scenic drive, winding around the magnificent Bras d'Or Lakes and mountains of the Island. The drive includes the resort town of Ingonish and Keltic Lodge, a deluxe hotel built on a cliff overlooking the sea.

One of the best museums on the east coast, the Alexander Graham Bell, celebrates the inventor of the telephone in the town where he spent his summers – Baddeck. Here, Bell spent most of his later life and conducted his many experiments in the area of flight.

Fortress Louisbourg on the Island, is Canada's largest and most absorbing historical recreation, 60 buildings in a walled town. It's a reincarnation of France's once-impregnable foothold in the New World, which twice fell to the British redcoats.

Those days are gone forever, and the only battles you'll see today are the lineups to get on the many ferries that service Atlantic Canada, including the *Bluenose* which sails from Yarmouth, N.S., to Bar Harbor, Maine.

There's also a ferry from Pictou, N.S., to Wood Islands, P.E.I. and a third from Saint John to the Nova Scotia resort town of Digby, home of the famous Pines Inn.

PRINCE EDWARD ISLAND

The major ferry service in the East, however, is from Cape Tormentine, N.B., to Borden, P.E.I., and provides hourly crossings during the summer when hundreds of thousands of tourists invade this tiny island province to sample everything from the warmest saltwater swimming in Canada to the famous lobster suppers.

P.E.I. really is a tourist paradise, and the Island works hard on the industry. The national parks of Cavendish and Stanhope are stunning, but the many provincial parks, offering fine beaches, camping and all the amenities, are nearly as good and far less crowded.

The capital of the Island is historic Charlottetown, known as the Cradle of Confederation because the first discussions of a union of British North America took place in Province House in September, 1864. One hundred years later, the province marked the event by opening its splashy new Confederation Centre, a huge complex that contains a theatre, restaurants and an art gallery.

The Charlottetown of today, more than 25,000 people, is a long way from that little French settlement of Port-la-Joie back in the 1500s. The name was changed to honor the consort of George III when the Island was ceded to Britain in 1763.

Now it's best known for the Charlottetown Summer Festival, a program of plays and musicals held each summer in the 946-seat Confederation Centre theatre. And the festival is best known for Anne of Green Gables, a musical about Lucy Maude Montgomery's little carrot-topped girl, that has been running to packed houses since 1965.

The city also has the fastest half-mile harness track in the East and bills itself as the Kentucky of Canada because the pacers and trotters go nightly in either Charlottetown or Summerside, just 34 miles down the Trans-Canada highway.

More than 500,000 people flock to the Island each summer, for the air, the swimming and the low prices. Tranquility still reigns here and the pace is slow. Beaches are miles long, all white or red sand, and the quiet lanes and sheltered coves provide solitude anywhere on the island.

Lobster is available across the Island and fishing is excellent, either for trout or in organized charters for the fast mackerel or mighty Bluefin tuna which can run up to 1,400 pounds. The island for years held the world record for the big fish.

Cavendish, or officially Prince Edward Island National Park, is the second most popular in Canada after Banff. It offers 40 kilometres of beaches, nature trails and fishing villages and is famous for Green Gables cottage, the setting for authoress Montgomery's books about Anne. Montgomery's birthplace is just up the road.

Nearby is the famous New Glasgow Community Hall where lobster suppers are served after 4 p.m. It is so popular that lineups form up to an hour before the doors open.

Summerside is the second biggest city on the Island and is the capital of Prince Country. It, like big brother Charlottetown, relies on tourism and fishing, especially oysters because Malpeque Bay is only a mile away.

In the east, there's the fishing village of Souris, which means mouse in French, and the agricultural town of Montague, one of the prettiest river locations in the province.

Close by is Brudenell Provincial Park, known for its golf course, camping and motel/hotel facilities and some of the island's best night life.

NEW BRUNSWICK
The Saint John River is the lifestream of New Brunswick, starting in the Loyalist City of Saint John itself on the Bay of Fundy and running north to capital city Fredericton and beyond into the Saint John Valley, where the wonderful meandering river provides beautiful scenery easily visible from the highway.

Saint John, founded in 1783 by hardy United Empire Loyalists, was incorporated in 1785, the year after the province itself was created. It set the tone for the new area, developing its lumber and shipbuilding industries and the port grew until today it is the commercial centre of the province.

There's heavy industry, pulp mills, sugar and oil refineries and, with 107,000 people, it is the largest centre in New Brunswick. It is also the site of the famous Reversing Falls, at the mouth of the Saint John River, which are one of the area's top tourist attractions.

Further up the river is beautiful little Fredericton, incorporated in 1848 and the seat of the province's legislature. It was the birthplace of poet Bliss Carman and industrialist Lord Beaverbrook, who has endowed the city with many museums, theatres and galleries.

It is also the home of the University of New Brunswick and Christ Church Cathedral, the first Anglican cathedral built in a new location since the Norman Conquest.

Today, it's a city of trees and quiet streets, lovely homes and lawns all flowing down to the river which dominates the area, which is an original pulp town known still for the warmest temperatures in the East.

Further north of Fredericton, hard by the State of Maine, is the Saint John River valley, rolling hills and winding blue water accented by dark green softwood ridges, fields of white potato blossoms and bright wild flowers.

But pull off the road and the rural routes are even more charming, areas like New Denmark which New Brunswickers call Brigadoon. The area was settled in 1872 by 29 Danes who came here to escape crop failures in their own country, and now mailboxes are studded with names like Hansen, Larsen, Pedersen and the soft lilt of the Danish language mingles with the aromas of frikadeller (meatballs).

In the north end of the province and the west French can become more prevalent than English in the fishing villages along the coast and the industrial cities of Bathurst and Campbellton, both close to the Quebec border.

Fundy National Park, along the Bay, in the south, is the foremost tourist attraction of the province, with warm water, acres of camping and wonderful scenery.

Nearby is the resort town of St. Andrews By The Sea and the Island of Campobello where FDR died. You can visit it today by boat, or sample the golf courses and famous inns of the area like the Rossmount, a Victorian renovation known for its preparation of fiddleheads, the delicious New Brunswick vegetable.

In the east, wending down the rocky coast to Cape Tormentine, lies the university town of Sackville (Mount Allison) which has developed into the province's main arts community, home to many well-known painters and scholars.

Moncton, with its booming airport, is the capital of eastern New Brunswick and the transportation centre of the Maritimes. It is also home to famous Magnetic Hill, a park just east of the city where cars appear to coast uphill instead of down – an optical illusion which has fooled everyone who has tried it.

But Moncton – an almost 50-50 mix of French and English – is also home to the Tidal Bore, a natural attraction caused by the rushing tide and easily seen from the many seafood restaurants that overlook the flats.

Atlantic Canada is still truly the place where men still go down to the sea in ships.

Colourful grain silos at Ponoka, Alberta.

Yukon

Above: a traditional husky dog sled picks a path across the frozen north. Facing page, top: the frozen waters of the Yukon River in Miles Canyon, a stretch of white water and dangerous swirls and eddies during the summer months. Facing page, bottom: houses in Whitehorse.

Whitehorse (these pages) came into being as a trans-shipment town for goods travelling the Yukon River; the violence of the river in Miles Canyon meant that goods had to be unloaded and carried on land past the obstruction. Fresh prosperity came with the railway in 1900, but the growth of the city's modern-day importance began with the Alaska Highway in 1942 and continued after the city became the territorial capital in 1953.

Facing page, top: the Alaska Highway, which was built in 1942 as an emergency war effort to get supplies to Alaska, south of Whitehorse. Facing page, bottom: the side road which leaves the Alaska Highway at Jakes Corner and heads south towards Atlin. Above: the Yukon River and Whitehorse.

Above: Whitehorse. Facing page, top: a road crosses the Yukon to run south along the east bank of the river to a point beyond Miles Canyon. Facing page, bottom: the *SS Klondike*, a restored sternwheeler which once carried passengers and ore along the river between Whitehorse and Dawson.

The sign in the image reads:

ISAAC O. STRINGER — "THE BISHOP WHO ATE HIS BOOTS"
A farm boy from Kincardine, Ontario, graduate of University of Toronto
and Wycliffe College, ordained in 1892 for Mackenzie River to serve
among Loucheaux Indians, Eskimo, and American whalers.
   Married Sarah Ann Alexander and ministered at Herschel Island until
snowblindness forced them to leave, in 1901.
   Came to Whitehorse in 1903, as rector. health improves.
   Elected second Bishop of Diocese in 1905, to succeed the aging
Bishop W.C. Bompas. 'The Apostle of the North'.
   In 1907 held first Diocesan Synod here:-moves See from
Fortymile to Dawson City -moves there himself. Serves next
25 years travelling far and wide as famous 'Bishop of Yukon'
1931-4 concludes life as Archbishop of Ruperts Land in Winnipeg.

Facing page, top: a ski-plane ready for use at Atlin. Facing page, bottom: the *SS Klondike* beside the Yukon River at Whitehorse. Above: Whitehorse's Old Log Church of 1900 on Elliott and Third. Overleaf: various scenes from Kluane National Park, which occupies 22,015 square kilometres of southwestern Yukon Territory.

41

Northwest Territories

Transport in the great spaces of the north traditionally relied on the husky-drawn sled (facing page, top) and whilst these are still used, modern methods such as ski-planes (above) have lessened the problem somewhat. Facing page, bottom: inflatable craft in Second Canyon of the Nahanni River.

These pages: Yellowknife is the capital of the Northwest Territories and lies on the northern shore of the Great Slave Lake. With an economy based on minerals, the city has a population approaching 9,000, making it the largest settlement in the Territories.

Facing page, top: a husky dog team waits for the musher to finalise his preparations prior to the start of an Arctic journey. Facing page, bottom: before the coming of Europeans the bulk of the 60-million-strong bison population lived on the great plains, but there were always small herds in the far north. Today, the Northwest Territories contain some of the few free-roaming animals left in the wild. Above: typical northern architecture.

Above: a snow-bound residential street in Yellowknife. Facing page, top: the buildings, equipment and sign of one of the mines outside Yellowknife. Linked to Yellowknife by a causeway, Latham Island (facing page, bottom) has houses perched above the lake and a Dogrib Indian settlement.

Facing page, top: a pick-up moves out of Detah towards the ice road to Yellowknife. Facing page, bottom: the Indian settlement on Latham Island. Above: a typical street scene in Yellowknife.

The future site of Yellowknife (these pages) was visited by three of the greatest explorers in the history of Canada: Samuel Hearne, Alexander Mackenzie and John Franklin, but none of them stayed. Permanent settlement had to wait until 1934 when gold was discovered and a boom town grew up.

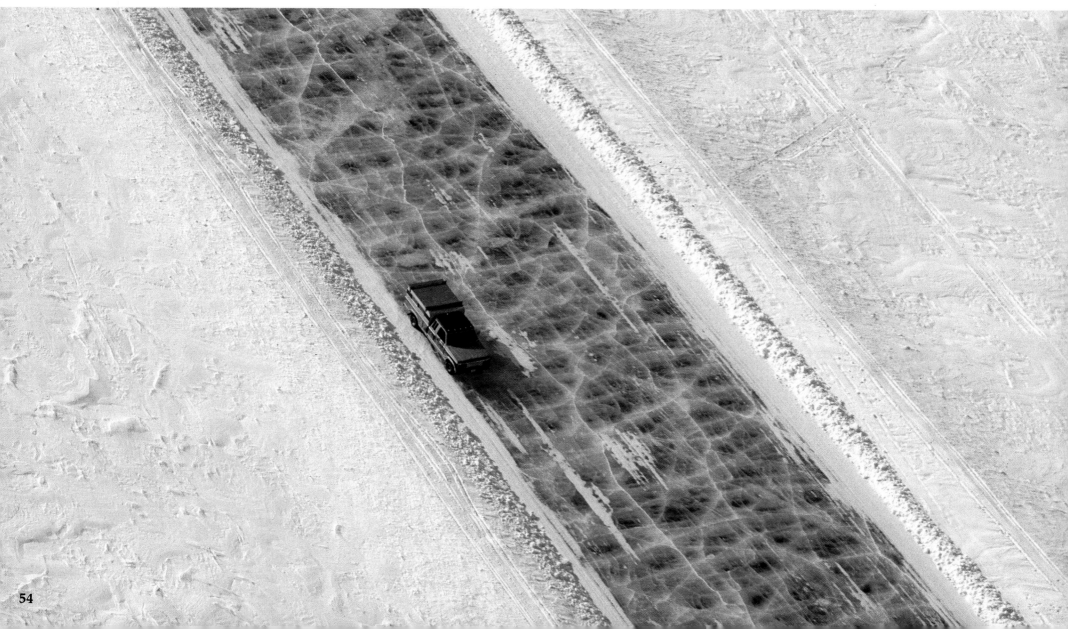

These pages: during the winter months, when the bitterly cold weather comes to Yellowknife, Yellowknife Bay, on the Great Slave Lake, freezes over to such a depth that the ice can carry the weight of motor vehicles across the lake, though it is often used for more light-hearted purposes.

Lying just south of the Arctic Circle, Yellowknife (these pages) does not quite achieve the midsummer sun of the far northern summer, instead it has a semi-dusk which persists past midnight into the early hours of the morning when the sun rises once again.

April or May are the ideal months to combine a weekend's camping trip by snowmobile (facing page) with some superb fishing for Arctic char in Baffin Island's many lakes, fiords or rivers. Above: the time-honoured method of igloo construction.

Although the hardy Inuit who inhabit the scattered communities of Baffin Island have adopted many modern ways, their lifestyle remains traditional to a surprising degree.

The rugged mountain peaks, which dominate the deep, glaciated valleys and fiords, (above) the Pangnirtung Fjord, draw climbers from around the world to Auyuittuq (these pages), the most northerly of Canada's national parks.

Sunset tints the ocean and the walls of ice at Cumberland Sound (above and facing page, top) where Inuit hunters look for seals. Seal meat forms part of the Inuit staple diet and the skins are used for clothing as well as being commercially marketed. Facing page, bottom: a dog enclosure.

Despite the advent of Western customs and practices, old skills and habits die hard, and the Inuit have retained the skills of igloo construction (facing page, top) and fishing with hook and line for Arctic char (above). Facing page, bottom: a traditionally clad Inuit child on the frozen surface of Pangnirtung Fjord.

Above: the time-honoured method of fishing for Arctic char in one of Baffin Island's many lakes.
Facing page, top: ice-bound fishing vessels in Frobisher Bay. Facing page, bottom: Pangnirtung Fjord
and the spectacular entrance to Auyuittuq National Park.

Above: an impatient dogteam prepares to leave Pangnirtung. Facing page: an Arctic sun sets over the frozen land (top), and visitors return from a day's exploration of Auyuittuq National Park (bottom).

Facing page, top: seal hunting in Cumberland Sound. Facing page, bottom: the return of a fishing expedition on the frozen surface of a river, and (above) running from a blizzard.

Facing page, bottom: marking out the base for an igloo prior to its construction (above). Facing page, top: floral-like crystals of ice decorate the floor of Auyuittuq National Park.

Facing page: the husky-drawn sled and motorised snowmobile; contrasting means of Arctic transportation. Above: an Inuit family fishes for char in the waters of a frozen lake.

Above: an appealing husky pup. Facing page, top: radio and tele-communications dishes on Baffin Island. Facing page, bottom: a polar bear skin drying outside a house in Pangnirtung.

Above: young visitor and Auyuittuq Park mascot. Facing page: snowmobiles on Baffin Island.

Timeless winter scenes on Baffin Island. Above: traditional Inuit clothing of caribou and sealskin.
Facing page: the frozen ocean (top) and a well-ordered team of huskies (bottom).

British Columbia

The elegant city of Victoria is the capital of British Columbia, and lends a graceful air to the western provinces. Among its more famous buildings are the Empress Hotel (facing page, top) of 1905 and the Parliament Buildings (above and facing page, bottom) built in the 1890s. Overleaf: (left) views along the province's coastline and (right) two liners, the *Queen of the North* and the *Prince George*, leaving Vancouver.

Facing page, top: pleasure boats at their moorings in Horseshoe Bay, starting point for a ferry to Vancouver Island. Facing page, bottom: the sun sets as a motor lauch hurries across Burrard Inlet in Vancouver. Above: the Lions Gate Bridge, which spans the First Narrows and links the city centre with North and West Vancouver. Overleaf: north of Vancouver the coast is heavily indented and dotted with small fishing villages.

Facing page, top: the sinking sun silhouettes a freighter in English Bay. Facing page, bottom: seen from North Vancouver, the Lions Gate Bridge appears deceptively rural in its surroundings. Above: the ship *Princess Patricia* moored in Coal Harbour.

Above: the forest of masts and maze of rigging of the Royal Vancouver Yacht Club. Facing page, top: small sailing craft beached at Kitsilano Yacht Club. Facing page, bottom: craft moored in Horseshoe Bay, where local Salish Indians astounded early explorers with the size of their canoes.

Facing page, top: two motor craft cross English Bay towards False Creek. Facing page, bottom: the orderly rows of moorings in False Creek Marina. Above: the mountain-dominated skyline of central Vancouver.

Facing page, top: Vancouver's skyline seen across Coal Harbour from Stanley Park. Facing page, bottom: the distinctive conical dome of the MacMillan Planetarium in Hadden Park. Above: the lights of central Vancouver. Overleaf: (top left and bottom right) the triodetic dome of the Bloedel Conservatory, set in the heart of Queen Elizabeth Park, and (top right and bottom left) the famous Butchart Gardens on the Saanich Peninsula of Vancouver Island.

Facing page, top: the trees of Stanley Park and the mountains beyond West Vancouver from the top of Harbour Centre. Facing page, bottom: the marina which lies in the shadow of Burrard Bridge and the city skyline. Above: the marina of the Royal Vancouver Yacht Club and the city skyline.

Facing page, bottom: the iron latticework of the bridges across False Creek. Facing page, top: Vancouverites enjoy the swimming pool at Kitsilano Beach. In 1867 John Deighton, known as Gassy Jack due to his talkativeness, opened a saloon by the mills on Burrard Inlet and gave his nickname to the town that sprang up around it. Today, Gastown (above) is an area of restored houses, shops, restaurants and import stores where the fashionable congregate.

Facing page, top: the city centre from Vanier Park. Facing page, bottom and above: the snow-capped peaks above Horseshoe Bay. Overleaf: (top left, top right and bottom right) some of the many marinas around the city and (bottom left) one of the multi-lane highways that keep the traffic moving.

Facing page, top: Vancouver from the top of the Harbour Centre. Facing page, bottom: a view from the crest of Granville Bridge, looking northeast along Granville Street. Above: the crowded moorings of False Creek Marina.

Strung along the west coast of Vancouver Island are the three separate areas of Pacific Rim National Park, established in 1970 to contain 388 square kilometres of beaches, rain-forest and coastal islands. Facing page, top: driftwood at low tide. Facing page, bottom: sunset over a tidal pool in Schooner Cove. Above: the mist-shrouded shoreline at Sealion Rocks.

Pacific Rim National Park was laid out to include as wide a variety of seashore and coastal habitats as possible. Facing page, top: sunset over Long Beach. Facing page, bottom: the rocky shore of the southernmost point of the Broken Group Islands. Above: the rain-forest at Long Beach.

Facing page, top: the fishing boat *Sea Buck* runs through the fog-shrouded waters of the Broken Group Islands. Facing page, bottom and above: driftwood on South Beach, Pacific Rim National Park.

Facing page, top: the purples and violets of dawn reflected in a tidal pool at Schooner Cove. Facing page, bottom: the foam-splattered rocks of Chesterman Beach. Above: sunset above the gently rolling sea at Green Point. Overleaf: (top left) the restored Main Street of Barkerville; (bottom left) reconstructed Fort Steele; (bottom right) the Prince George Professional Rodeo and (top right) a Pacific Coast Indian totem pole at the Victoria Heritage Court Complex.

These pages: views of the Rockies near Squamish.

These pages: the snow-clad Rockies between Squamish and Mount Whistler.

Facing page, top: a mountain lake in Yoho National Park. Facing page, bottom: Schaeffer Lake, surrounded by brooding, snow-clad peaks. Above: a train entering the spiral tunnel under Mount Ogden, built in 1909 to reduce the gradient of the railway tracks over Kicking Horse Pass.

Facing page, top: the snows of autumn blanket the Mount Odaray Plateau Grand View. Facing page, bottom: the bulk of 3,199-metre-tall Mount Stephen towers over Kicking Horse Valley. Above: Lake Oesa, ringed by Mounts Lefroy and Yukness. Overleaf: (top left) a moose; (top right and bottom left) deer and (bottom right) a coyote.

Facing page, top: the snow-clad scene at Mount Odaray Plateau Grand View. Facing page, bottom: the impressive cascade of the Wapta Falls. Above: the small town of Field, which lies near the eastern end of Kicking Horse Pass. Overleaf: (top left) the CN railway crossing the North Thompson River near the town of Blue River; (bottom left) the fertile Okanagan Valley; (top right) the lofty mountains behind the Skeena River and (bottom right) Pavilion Lake near Lillooet.

Facing page, top: tree-clad slopes between Squamish and Mount Whistler. Set in a provincial park of its own, the triangular peak of Mount Assiniboine, seen on the skyline (facing page, bottom) is surrounded by some of the most spectacular scenery in the province (above).

Above: a rural scene viewed from the Trans-Canada Highway near Prince George. Facing page, top: Mount Whistler Ski Resort. Facing page, bottom: one of the ski centres near Mount Whistler.

Facing page, top: the jagged, shark-toothed peak of Mount Assiniboine amid neighbouring mountains.
Facing page, bottom: the Rockies between Squamish and Mount Whistler. Above: a frozen lake near
Squamish.

Above: Horseshoe Bay at sunset. Facing page, top: the silky waters of a northern mountain lake.
Facing page, bottom: a band of cloud drifts across the face of Mount Robson.

Facing page, top: Mount Assiniboine and surrounding peaks. Facing page, bottom and above: the towering face of Mount Robson, one of the most impressive mountains in the province.

Facing page, top: the chair-lift and wooded slopes of the popular Mount Whistler Ski Resort. Facing page, bottom and above: aerial views of the Rockies around Mount Whistler.

These pages: Mount Revelstoke National Park was created in 1914 to encompass a unique series of rain-forest-covered valleys, Alpine slopes and cold mountain peaks. One of the more informative aspects of the park is the Giant Cedars Trail (above) in one the valleys.

In 1968 a great forest fire swept along the Vermilion Pass, leaving a trail of dead tree trunks and
ravaged countryside (facing page, bottom). Even today the young trees amid the skeletal trunks reach
no higher than a moose's shoulder (facing page, top). Above: Mount Harkin and neighbouring peaks.
Overleaf: (top left) Muncho Lake on the Alaska Highway; (bottom left) Bowron Lake; (top right) the
Alaska Highway beyond Wonowon and (bottom right) the Okanagan Valley.

Alberta

Facing page, top: the scattered township of Canmore, a fishing centre near Banff National Park.
Facing page, bottom: Highway 93 snakes along a valley near Banff. Above: an interchange on the
Trans-Canada Highway near Canmore.

Facing page, top: a mule deer, perhaps the commonest deer in the western provinces, feeding in the snows of Jasper National Park. Facing page, bottom: a bull elk, at 5 feet tall one of the largest deer in North America. Above: an aerial view of Banff with the Upper Hot Springs in the clearing in the foreground.

Facing page, top: the forested slopes around Banff. Facing page, bottom: the Bow River near Banff. Above: the divided course of the Bow River, the edifice of the Banff Springs Hotel and the sprawling streets of Banff townsite.

Facing page, top: adventurous hikers make their way up towards the Columbia Icefields. Facing page, bottom: benches on the frozen surface of Lake Louise, northwest of Banff. Above: the Rockies near Banff.

Lake Louise (these pages) is one of the most popular areas in the Rockies with both visitors and photographers. The lake is backed by the mountains of the Continental Divide and offers visitors a whole range of summer and winter sports facilities from the Chateau Lake Louise Hotel (above).

Facing page, top: the Bow River flows between frozen banks near Lake Louise. Facing page, bottom: the snow-covered peaks of the Colorado Rockies. Above: the sheer face of Mount Eisenhower, said by Indians to be the home of the Chinook.

Facing page, top: a view of Tunnel Mountain, Cascade Mountain and Banff townsite from the top of Mount Sulphur. Facing page, bottom: the circular platform of the terminal of the Mount Sulphur gondola rises above Banff. Above: the frozen Spray Lakes Reservoir, near Banff.

Facing page, top: a river near the Yellowhead Pass. Facing page, bottom: the town of Jasper, which serves the national park of that name. The town began as a way station for trappers, surveyors and prospectors in the last century, only opening for park visitors in 1915. Above: the smooth flow of the Athabasca River in Jasper National Park.

Facing page, top: a farm building beside the Yellowhead Highway, west of Jasper. Facing page, bottom: the ice-fringed Athabasca River in Jasper National Park. Above: horses grazing amid the snows of Jasper National Park.

Facing page, top: the chairlift at the Sunshine Ski Resort. The area in which stands the Lake Louise Ski Resort (facing page, bottom and above) was unknown to Europeans until local Indians led Tom Wilson, a CPR man, there in 1882. Overleaf: (top left) a snow-covered scene near Edmonton; (bottom left) farm buildings outside Edmonton; (top right) the Edmonton skyline and (bottom right) the ice-rink in West Edmonton Mall.

Facing page, top: wildflowers and (facing page, bottom) fields of waving grain on the Albertan prairies. Above: a mule deer on the shores of Medicine Lake.

When the American bison (these pages) had the run of the prairies from the Gulf of Mexico to the Arctic Circle they moved in herds numbered in tens of thousands. Today, the preserved population of bison is barely one tenth of one per cent of the original wild population.

Facing page, top: the Trans-Canada Highway running west from Calgary towards the mountains of Banff National Park. Facing page, bottom and above: the soaring skyline of Calgary, a town which began its oil business in a big way when Digman No.1 produced the precious liquid in 1914.

Facing page, top: the Bow River and the skyline of Calgary. Facing page, bottom: the frozen surface of Bow Lake and the surrounding mountains in which the Bow River has its source. Above: west of Calgary flows the Kananaskis River, a tributary of the Bow.

These pages: around the town of Banff rise the majestic peaks of the Colorado Rockies.

Facing page: two views of the sharp peaks and forested slopes of the Colorado Rockies. Above: farm buildings on the Trans-Canada Highway near Calgary, dominated by the mountains beyond.

The Muttart Conservatory, on the south bank of the North Saskatchewan River, consists of four glass pyramids in which are kept plants from three different climates, and forms one of Edmonton's most popular attractions.

Facing page, top: the famous sculpture *Family of Man* by Mario Armengol, which stands outside Calgary's Education Centre. Facing page, bottom: central Edmonton. Above: the Legislative Building, which overlooks the North Saskatchewan River and was built of Quebec, Pennsylvanian and Italian marble in 1912.

The Stampede which hits Calgary for ten days every July advertises itself as the Greatest Dad Burned Show on Earth. A favourite feature of the show is the bronc-busting (these pages), which is also one of the more exciting events.

Facing page, top: a chuck-wagon race. Facing page, bottom: Indians in colourful bead-worked garb.
Above: one of the more hair-raising events at the Stampede is calf-wrestling, in which a running
calf must be brought to the ground by muscle power alone.

The rich farmlands of Alberta are epitomised at Fairview (facing page, top) and Beaverlodge (facing page, bottom). Above: a mass of low cloud threatens to engulf the Athabasca River as it flows between forested banks.

Facing page, bottom: a meltwater stream leaves the Columbia Icefield, whence the Athabasca River (facing page, top) draws its headwaters before flowing to the Arctic Ocean. Above: sunset over a quiet Albertan lake.

Facing page, top: hoodoos in Dinosaur Valley, near Drumheller. The Valley earned its peculiar name from the enormous number of dinosaur fossils which have been discovered in its rocks, including one that scientists have named *Edmontosaurus*. Facing page, bottom: Horsethief Canyon, near Drumheller. Above: the bare landscape of Writing-on-Stone Provincial Park.

Above and facing page, top: in the extreme west of Alberta lies Medicine Lake, so named for its apparently magical properties. For much of the year the lake is a bed of dry gravel, until the spring thaw fills it with water which then seeps away to join the Maligne River through no visible route. Facing page, bottom: the mountains of Banff National Park.

Facing page, top: a snow-clad peak near Banff. Facing page, bottom: the mass of Mount Rundle looms above Banff townsite. Above: the silky surface of Peyto Lake, named after Bill Peyto, a mountain man and later a park warden in the Banff region.

Facing page, top: natural rock pillars overlook a valley just to the east of Banff. Facing page, bottom: the rippling waters of Lake Louise in winter. Above: a thin sheet of ice spreads across Moraine Lake in the Valley of the Ten Peaks.

Facing page, top: Buffalo Paddock in Waterton Lakes National Park. Facing page, bottom: the southern peaks of the Canadian Rockies lie reflected in a waterhole at Twin Buttes. Above: part of the largest free-roaming bison herd in Canada, in Wood Buffalo National Park.

Facing page, top: Maligne Lake, which was originally named Sore-foot Lake by Henry Macleod when he discovered it in 1875. Facing page, bottom: water runs off the rocks of Maligne Canyon. Above: a tiny, tree-covered islet on Maligne Lake.

Facing page, top: the waters of a stream in Red Rock Canyon, in the Blakiston Valley, flow over a multi-coloured bed. Facing page, bottom: bison graze the prairie in southwestern Alberta. Above: Vimy Ridge (left) and Mount Richards (right) reflected in Maskinonge Lake.

Facing page, top: Angel Glacier, on the slopes of Mount Edith Cavell, just catches the first rays of morning sunlight. Facing page, bottom and above: the jumble of ice that is the Athabasca Glacier, at the southern end of Jasper National Park.

Facing page, top: Lake Cameron, in the southwest of the province. Facing page, bottom: Tunnel Mountain and its much larger neighbour, Mount Rundle, seen from the west. Above: the Prince of Wales Hotel in Waterton Lakes National Park.

218

Elk Island National Park (these pages) is one of the smallest national parks in the country, yet some 35 species of mammal find a home in the park which originated as a preserve in the Beaver Hills in 1906.

Facing page, top: the deserted Icefields Parkway near Lake Louise. Facing page, bottom: chair-lifts at the Sunshine Ski Resort. Above: Cirrus Mountain and Sunwapta Pass, near the headwaters of the North Saskatchewan River.

Saskatchewan

A threatening sky (above) hangs over Saskatchewan's prairielands, part of which have been set aside to form Grasslands National Park (these pages). Despite their severe winters and sweltering summers, the province's plains remain one of the nation's most productive agricultural regions.

The ground squirrel (above), chipmunk (facing page, bottom) and wapiti (facing page, top); three of Saskatchewan's many animal species.

Wind-rippled lakes (facing page, bottom), dense stands of trembling aspen and balsam poplar (facing page, top) and (above) frost-crisped conifer woods; all are representative of the Saskatchewan landscape.

Although known as a prairie province, much of low-lying Saskatchewan consists of lake and woodland as well as poorly drained bush, as evidenced by the views (these pages) of Prince Albert National Park, which lies at the heart of the province.

With no mountains and few hills of any appreciable size to interrupt the distant view, Saskatchewan's sobriquet of 'big sky country' is a particularly appropriate one. The province's undulating plains (these pages), with their distinctive grain elevators (above), provide more than half of Canada's grain yield.

Founded in 1882 as Pile of Bones, on account of the bleached buffalo remains found in the area, the city of Regina was renamed in 1905 when it became the capital of the province of Saskatchewan. The city, with its elegant Legislative Building (above) and futuristic New City Hall (facing page, top), is among the fastest growing in the country. Facing page, bottom: newly harvested prairie wheatfield.

Plains bison (facing page, top) and the industrious beaver (above) are among the animal inhabitants of Prince Albert National Park where, on the shores of Ajawaan Lake, is found the cabin (facing page, bottom) as well as the burial place of the famous naturalist writer Grey Owl.

Above: reeds grow at the edge of a roadside pond near the Heart Lakes. Facing page, top: King Island, seen across the placid waters of Waskesiu Lake. Facing page, bottom: lightning rends the sky over Halkett Lake.

A grazing bull moose (facing page, bottom) and a wary snowshoe hare (facing page, top) are among the more commonly encountered inhabitants in the region of the slow flowing Waskesiu River (above), in Saskatchewan's Prince Albert National Park.

Facing page, top: a beaver and (above) its lodge at the edge of Amiskowan Lake, and (facing page, bottom) a fiery sunset over Waskesiu Lake, Prince Albert National Park.

The inoffensive and distinctive-looking mule deer (above) is common to many parts of Canada west of Manitoba, while the prairie garter snake and prairie rattlesnake, as their names suggest, are reptiles native to the plains.

Manitoba

For approximately three months of the year, the small town of Churchill becomes a bustling seaport, its elevators (above) storing the Manitoban grain that is destined for all corners of the world. In winter, with the Hudson Bay impassable to ships, the landscape around the town (facing page) takes on a bleak appearance.

A pale, winter dawn rises over Churchill (facing page, bottom) and the ice-bound Churchill River (facing page, top). Although the town appears deserted and isolated, the rail lines (above) maintain its link with the rest of the province.

Facing page: Churchill's railway station (top) and its still harbour (bottom). Freezing conditions ensure that outdoor activities are kept to a minimum and frequently the only sign of life may be the smoke from the town's chimneys (above).

Above: a desolate view of the Churchill River. Facing page: a forest of telegraph posts along Kelsey Boulevard (top), and (bottom) a tug imprisoned in the frozen waters of Churchill harbour.

252

Originally a fur trading post founded in 1685 by the Hudson's Bay Company, Churchill (these pages) gained in importance with the arrival of the railway in 1931 and the building of the port facilities shortly thereafter.

The magnificent Neo-Classical Manitoba Legislative Building (these pages), topped by the famous 'Golden Boy' statue, stands amid a welter of modern buildings that reflect the importance of cosmopolitan Winnipeg.

Stretching uninterrupted to the distant horizon, Manitoba's fertile southern farmlands (these pages) are a major source of her prosperity.

Facing page, top: a patchwork of fields at the 40-acre Mennonite Village Museum at Steinbach. Facing page, bottom: campers by the shores of Two Mile Lake, in Duck Mountain Provincial Park. Above: autumn's russet hues tint the Manitoban woodland scene.

Ontario

Above: the frozen surface of Lake Superior at Thunder Bay. The city of Thunder Bay was created in 1970 as an amalgam of the neighbouring communities of Port Arthur and Fort William. From Port Arthur (facing page, top) can be seen the mass of the Sleeping Giant, which lies on the peninsula across the Bay. Facing page, bottom: an Ontario farm near Thunder Bay.

Thunder Bay (these pages), on the shores of Lake Superior, is a major industrial city and one of
Canada's largest ports, where Prairie wheat is stored in the huge elevators (facing page, top) prior
to shipment via the St. Lawrence Seaway. The docks also handle much of Ontario's important mineral
output as well as the produce from industries such as Thunder Bay's own Great Lakes Paper Mill
(facing page, bottom).

These pages: the nail-biting excitement of the Canadian Ski Jumping Championships at Thunder Bay.

Located on the shores of Lake Superior, Pukaskwa National Park is an unspoilt wilderness area within whose boundaries can be found a wealth of scenery: from debris-strewn beaches (facing page, top) and views across the lake as near Horseshoe Beach (facing page, bottom), to the Boreal Forest on Southern Headland (above).

The woodlands of St. Lawrence Islands National Park are the habitat of a variety of colourful flowers, including the delicate wood lily (above), the hairy beardtongue (facing page, top) and the insectivorous pitcher plant (facing page, bottom).

Above: a shady woodland trail near Castle Bluff, on Flowerpot Island; (facing page, top) sun dappled scene on Beausoleil Island and (facing page, bottom) the smooth, rocky foreshore at Finger Point, all in Georgian Bay Islands National Park.

Point Pelee National Park (these pages), in southwestern Ontario, an area of marsh and woodland rich in rare plant and birdlife, stands at the tip of a sandy peninsula on the shores of Lake Erie and enjoys some of Canada's warmest weather.

These pages: scenes from the Great Lakes region of Ontario, whose most awesome spectacle is surely the spray enshrouded precipice of the Niagara Falls (above).

Suitably attired sightseers can enjoy the full splendour of the Falls from below by taking a trip aboard one of the *Maid of the Mist* boats (facing page). Above: a bird's eye view of the turbulent waters of Horseshoe Falls.

The solid curtain of water that crashes over Niagara Falls (these pages) suffuses the air with a constant roar. At night and during the winter their volume decreases as some of the flow is diverted to generate electricity.

The vibrant city of Toronto, with its world famous CN Tower and the space-age Ontario Place (above), is Canada's prime business and industrial centre as well as her largest metropolis. Facing page, top: the Ice Canoe Race across the frozen waters of the Harbour during the Molson Winterfest celebrations. Facing page, bottom: the outlines of Toronto's highrise office blocks seen across the sunset-gilded waters of the Harbour.

The magnificent Eaton Centre (these pages), which stands on Yonge Street and sprawls over several blocks in central Toronto, houses over 300 fine shops, stores and restaurants on three levels, all enclosed by an arched glass roof.

Above: the high-rise towers of Toronto's business district at twilight. Facing page, top: the start of the exciting Ice Canoe Race, one of the events during the Winterfest festival. Facing page, bottom: scavenging gulls wheel over the waters of the Harbour.

The world's tallest free-standing structure, Toronto's CN Tower (above) offers superlative views from its Space Deck. Facing page: neat, colourful gardens on Toronto Islands, one of the city's prime summer playgrounds (top), and Ontario Place and Marina (bottom).

Hailed as an architectural masterpiece, Viljo Revell's Toronto City Hall (above), which stands in Nathan Phillips Square, superseded its predecessor, neighbouring Old City Hall (facing page, bottom), in 1965. Facing page, top: the Toronto Islands ferry, which links the city with the parkland to the south.

Among Toronto's varied attractions is the ornate Casa Loma (above), built by financier Sir Henry Pellatt in 1914, and the futuristic Ontario Place (facing page, top), a summertime entertainment complex that houses theatres, cinema, outdoor concert hall and children's playground. Nathan Phillips Square also regularly hosts events, such as the performance by the Police Pipe Band (facing page, bottom).

Ontario's squat Parliament Building (above) stands within the confines of Queen's Park and is flanked by government buildings to the right and the curved tower of the Ontario Hydro headquarters shown bottom left. Facing page: Toronto Islands ferry (top), and the soaring spire of the CN Tower (bottom).

Foremost among Toronto's many examples of fine modern architecture are the gold coloured triangular towers of the Royal Bank Plaza (facing page, top), the famous City Hall (facing page, bottom) and the Harbourfront development (above).

Facing page, top: University Avenue looking north towards the Ontario Legislative Building in Queen's Park (facing page, bottom). Above: the city and CN Tower seen from the railway sidings in the Waterfront area.

Toronto's Ontario Place (facing page) and Eaton Centre (above) are just two of the many attractions
in this bustling and most cosmopolitan of Canadian cities.

When construction of Kingston's fine City Hall (above) first began in the 1840s it was anticipated that the building would house the parliament of Upper and Lower Canada, but the capital was moved to Montreal before the work was completed. Facing page: freighters in the Soo Locks at Sault Ste. Marie on the Saint Lawrence Seaway (top), and (bottom) one of International Nickel's huge processing plants in Ontario.

Standing on Hill Island between the spans of the Thousand Islands International Bridge (facing page, top), the Thousand Islands Skydeck offers superb views of the region (above) from its observation deck. Among the many islands in this stretch of the St. Lawrence is Heart Island (facing page, bottom), on which stands the castle built by millionaire George Boldt for his wife.

Above: the Thousand Islands International Bridge, opened in 1938 by Prime Minister Mackenzie King and President Roosevelt, links Ivy Lea, Ontario, with Collins Landing in New York state. Facing page: the Skydeck observation tower on Hill Island (top), and the bridge over Sioux Narrows, Lake of the Woods, which extends across western Ontario and into Manitoba (bottom).

Above: a tranquil sunset over Lake Superior. Facing page: a timeless river scene in Pukaskwa National Park (top), and (bottom) a tanker passes under the Ogdensburg-Prescott International Bridge, near Johnstown.

Above and facing page, bottom: autumn's mellow red and russet hues paint the Ontario landscape by the Rideau Canal. Facing page, top: boulder-strewn rapids in the aptly-named Rushing River Provincial Park.

Ottawa's Gothic-style Parliament Building (these pages) overlooks the city from its elevated position on Parliament Hill. The three blocks are dominated by the lofty Peace Tower (above), which was added in 1927 as a monument to the Canadians who died in the First World War.

The ornate Senate Chamber (facing page, top), with its murals recalling scenes from the Great War, is located in the Centre Block of the Parliament Buildings (facing page, bottom), as is the vaulted Confederation Hall (above).

The resemblance of Ottawa's many-spired Houses of Parliament (above and facing page, bottom) to the Houses of Parliament in London lends meaning to the city's long-standing sobriquet of 'Westminster of the Wilderness.' Facing page, top: a sleigh ride on the frozen Dows Lake during the annual Winterlude festivities.

The magnificent Chateau Laurier (these pages), built in the style of a French chateau, stands across the Rideau Canal from the Parliament Buildings and is one of the city's finest and most distinctive hotels. Facing page, top: the hotel seen from Major's Hill Park.

The Rideau Canal (above), which runs through the heart of Ottawa, provides year-round recreational facilities; in summer pleasure craft are to be seen moored to the banks, while in winter a seven-kilometre stretch of the waterway serves as a much-used skating rink. Far from driving the inhabitants indoors, winters are a time of celebration, with Winterlude, which includes such events as husky team competitions (facing page, bottom), being a major Ottawa occasion each February.

These pages: the Blue Mountains near Collingwood (these pages), north of Toronto, offer some of the best Alpine skiing facilities in the region.

Quebec

In winter the spectacular Falls of the Montmorency River (above), near where it joins the mighty St. Lawrence, create a spectacular ice cone that has been known to rise to over 70 feet in height.
Facing page: ski slopes at Mont-Ste-Anne (top), and Stoneham Ski Resort (bottom).

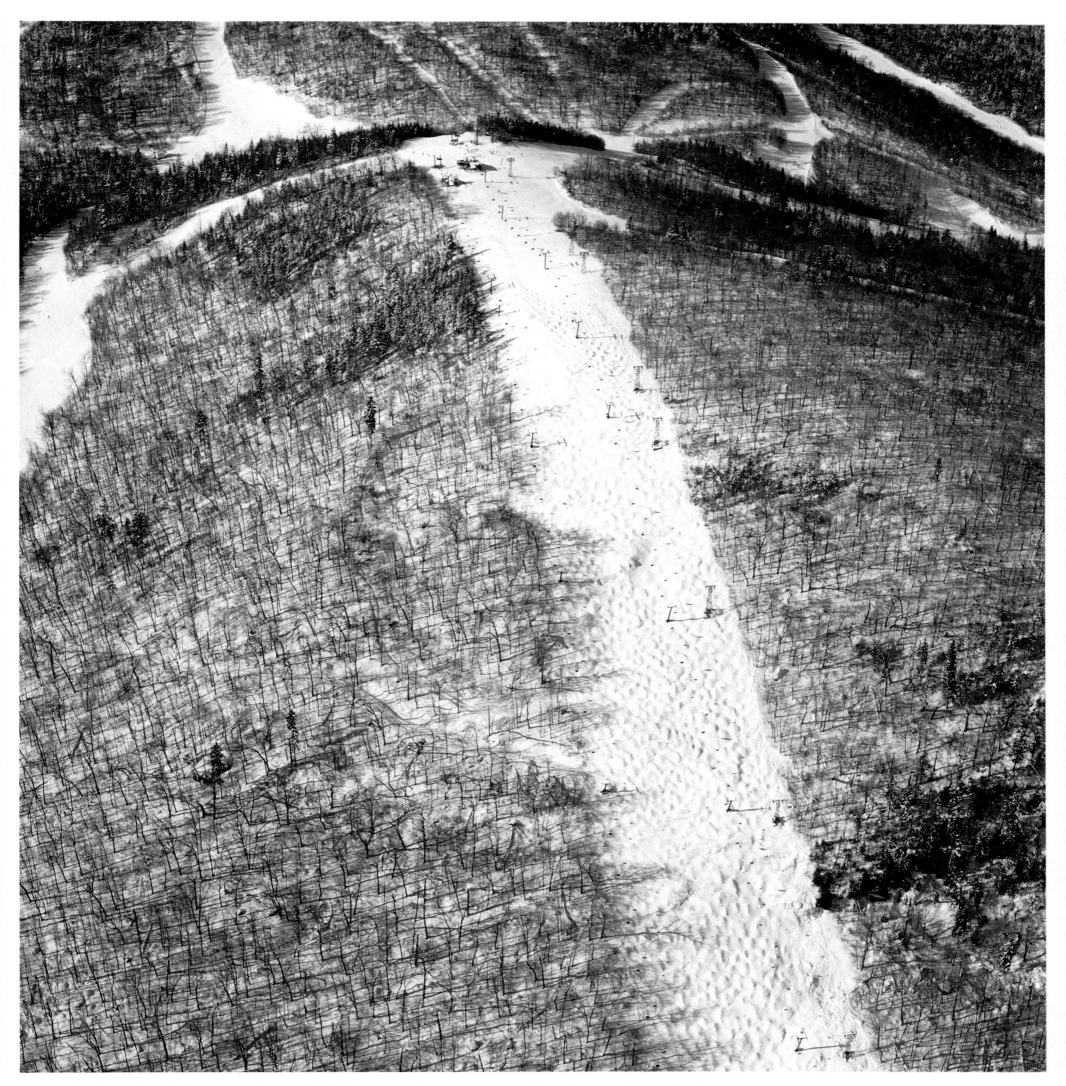

A multitude of downhill runs and some 130 kilometres of cross-country ski trails make Mont-Ste-Anne (these pages) one of eastern Canada's finest regions for winter sports.

Turreted Chateau Frontenac (above), set within Quebec's city walls, overlooks the lighthouse on
Champlain Boulevard. Facing page: ice sculpture (top) and a canoe race across the partially frozen
St. Lawrence River (bottom) are just two of the events during the annual 'Carnaval' winter carnival.

Dufferin Terrace and the Chateau Frontenac Hotel (above) are accessible by funicular from the Lower
Town. Within the walls of the city can be seen the Citadel (facing page, top), which was built by
the British in anticipation of attack by American forces. Facing page, bottom: the city's twin
bridges: the Pierre Laporte (right) and Quebec Bridge (left).

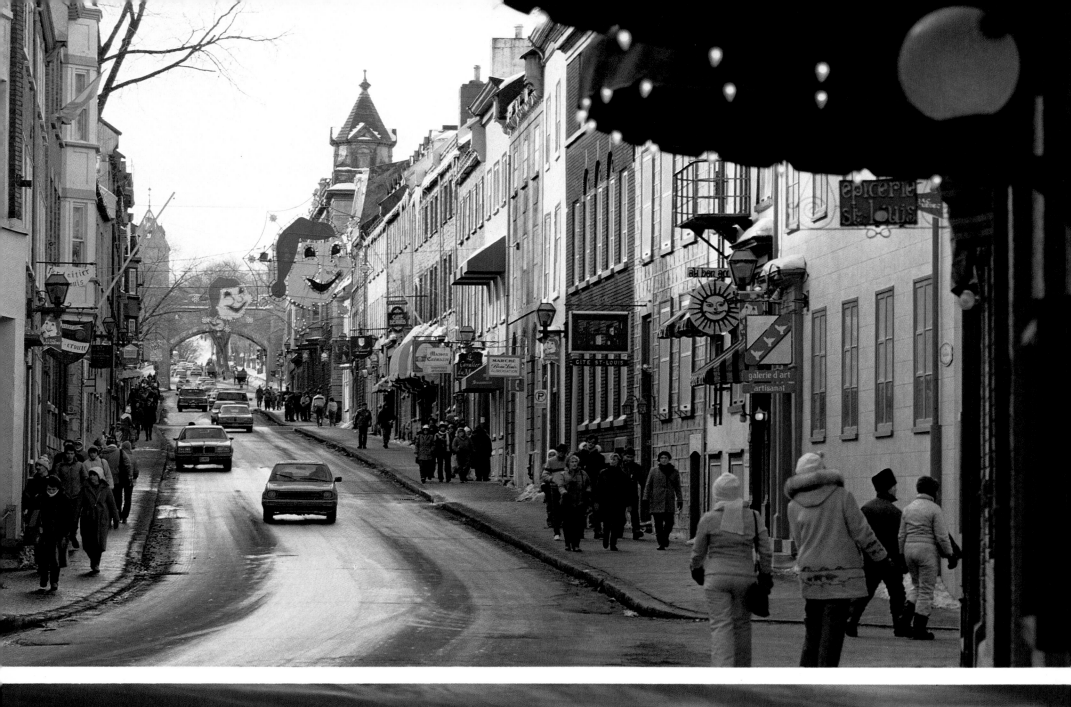

Facing page, top: jovial snowmen decorate Quebec City's Rue St-Louis at Carnaval time. Facing page, bottom: the lights of the new city from the heights of the Old City. Above: a lonely figure in the slush-strewn Rue Petit Champlain in the Lower Town of Quebec.

Facing page: ice sculptures on Dufferin Avenue, during February's 'Carnaval'. Above: the Upper Town, with the Citadel walls in the foreground, and the docks and industrial area on the St. Charles River beyond.

Facing page, top: the Chateau Frontenac Hotel from Dufferin Terrace. Facing page, bottom: the Legislative Building stands beyond the green ditch which surrounds the city walls. Above: the Chateau Frontenac from the lighthouse by the St. Lawrence.

Magnificently sited high above the St. Lawrence River
and Lower Town, the gracious Chateau Frontenac Hotel
(these pages) offers its guests incomparable views of
Quebec and the historic Citadel and Plains of Abraham
to the south (facing page top).

Above: the green-roofed Chateau Frontenac, built in 1893, stands out against the snow-covered Upper Town. Facing page: two of the colourful floats which take part in the procession during Carnaval.

Facing page, top: the Chateau Frontenac overlooks the Lower Town. Facing page, bottom: bright lights illuminate the snow palace and snow sculptures beside the Porte St-Louis, as part of the Carnaval celebrations. Above: the green-roofed Holy Trinity Anglican Cathedral of 1804.

These pages: Montreal is the largest city in the province, with 2.5 million in the greater city and has long been a leading centre for industry, trade and finance, a role it continues to fulfil to this day.

Facing page, top: the summit of snow-covered Mont Tremblant, which towers over Mont-Tremblant-Village and the frozen waters of Lac Tremblant (above). Facing page, bottom: the Gray Rocks Resort northeast of Montreal.

Facing page, top: the snow-bound resort of Gray Rocks, near St-Jovite. Facing page, bottom: broad roads sweep through Sainte-Agathe-des-Monts, north of Montreal. Above: children on a chair-lift ascend the slopes of Mont Tremblant.

Facing page, top: the near-deserted slopes of Mont Tremblant, which rise above the red-roofed church (above). Facing page, bottom: scenery southwest of St-Jovite.

North of Trois-Rivières lie the 544 square kilometres of La Mauricie National Park (these pages), a region of dense forests, steep hills and open lakes which are said to number over 150.

Facing page, top: a riot of autumnal colours blankets the slopes at Lac à Saur. Facing page, bottom: a well-organised interpretive canoe trip on a lake in La Mauricie National Park. Above: a surf-boarder on Lac Edouard, in the southern half of the park.

The scenic tourist village of Percé, once the largest fishing village in the area, lies at the tip of Quebec's spectacularly rugged Gaspé Peninsula (these pages) and takes its name from the enormous eroded red limestone rock that lies just offshore.

Newfoundland

Facing page, top: the town of Placentia, which was a French stronghold during the 17th century.
Facing page, bottom: Heart's Content where, in 1866, the *Great Eastern* landed the western end of the
first successful transatlantic telegraph cable. Above: St. John's, the magnificent capital of
Newfoundland, which began as a fishing station soon after John Cabot's voyages.

Facing page, top: a fishing village near Twillingate. Facing page, bottom: Bonavista, where stands a statue of John Cabot to commemorate his landfall at Cape Bonavista in 1497. Above: Pouch Cove, whose orginal settlers of 1611 chose the dangerous harbour for its inaccessibility to government agents, settlement in Newfoundland being illegal at that time.

The spectacular, 600-metre-tall cliffs which surround Western Brook Pond (facing page) are the result of grinding glacier action during the last great ice age. Above: the tranquil waters of Lobster Cove, overshadowed by the cliffs of Green Gardens.

Gros Morne National Park (these pages) lies along the west coast of Newfoundland and contains some of the most geologically interesting landforms in the country, as well as some of the best fishing rivers (facing page, top). Facing page, bottom: Lobster Cove Head Lighthouse. Above: the might of Bakers Brook Falls.

Facing page, top: an iceberg drifting offshore at Bonavista. Facing page, bottom: seaside houses near Twillingate. Above: small boats moored in Quidi Vidi Village.

Above: the 5,239-foot-long A. Murray MacKay bridge which spans The Narrows in Halifax. Facing page, bottom: the tiny fishing village of Peggy's Cove and (facing page, top) nearby scenery.

Halifax (facing page, bottom) preserves much of its past in the Historic Properties (facing page, top and above), east of Lower Water Street, where wharehouses, quays and ships are lovingly cared for and people can relax.

Facing page, top: the oldest building in Halifax is Saint Paul's church, which was built in 1750 and was once the cathedral of the diocese of Nova Scotia. Facing page, bottom: the Halifax Public Gardens, first opened in 1867. Above: Water Street in St. Andrews.

The star shaped Citadel (above and facing page, bottom) which dominates Halifax (these pages) was built in 1828 to defend the city from foreign attack. Today, the fortress is used as a museum, and costumed staff recreate the drill and manoeuvres of the troops who once manned the Citadel.

Facing page, top: the gentle Joe Howe Falls in Victoria Park, Truro. Facing page, bottom and above: the Mersey River in Kejimkujik National Park is ideal for canoeists and lovers of outdoor life.

These pages: Peggy's Cove stands on the rocky shore at the mouth of St. Margaret's Bay, where the road from Halifax loops north towards Upper Tantallon. Its tiny population seems to remain almost unaffected by the hordes of tourists and artists who descend on their village throughout the year.

Above: Peggy's Cove. Facing page, top: Glace Bay, which received its name from early French arrivals who found ice, or *glace* in the bay. Facing page, bottom: a boat enters Sandford Harbour on the province's west coast.

Facing page, top: low tide reveals a weed-strewn shore at Broad Cove, on the southwest coast of the province. Facing page, bottom and above: Blue Rocks, a charming village of clapboard houses near Lunenburg.

Facing page, top: Cape St. Mary, at the entrance to St. Mary's Bay on the west coast. Facing page, bottom: the lobster pots and lighthouse of Neil's Harbour, which stands on the coast near Cape Breton Highlands National Park. Above: the fishing village of Tiverton, at the seaward end of the Bay of Fundy.

These pages: Peggy's Cove, one of the most delightful and charming fishing villages in Nova Scotia.

Prince Edward Island

Facing page, top: the old farmhouse in Cavendish which served as a model for the home of Anne of Green Gables in Lucy Maud Montgomery's famous novel of that name. Facing page, bottom: Charlottetown's Government House, which was erected in 1834 and serves as the home of the Lieutenant Governor. Above: North Rustico Harbour.

Above: a piper plover staunchly guards its egg and chick in the sand. Facing page, top: the red cliffs of Orby Head. Facing page, bottom: one of the numerous sandy beaches which make Prince Edward Island so popular with bathers.

Above: the windswept Stanhope Cape Lighthouse. Facing page: some of the livestock which form such an important part of the provincial economy.

New Brunswick

The refurbished Market Square (these pages) in Saint John, largest city of New Brunswick.

Above: the mill at Kings Landing Historical Settlement. Facing page, top: the Point Wolfe covered bridge and dam. Facing page, bottom: a bathing beach near Saint John.

Above: the interior of the restored Officers' Quarters in Fredericton's Military Compound. Facing page: Kings Landing Historical Settlement, with over 60 buildings, is an authentic reconstruction of the past.

When the Mactaquac Dam was threatening to inundate large areas of the Saint John River valley it was decided to move some of the more historically important buildings to a new and safer site. Consequently, Kings Landing Historical Settlement (these pages) came into being on a 121-hectare site, some 22 kilometres upstream from Fredericton on the Saint John River. Not only are the bare buildings of days gone by seen here; the costumed staff work the farms and machinery to create an exciting and authentic atmosphere.

Above: the gushing waters of Dickson Falls in Fundy National Park.